EGE   T400
        41.56E
        TAC

THE TIMES

FOOD FOR FEASTS
AND FESTIVALS

THE TIMES
FOOD FOR FEASTS
AND FESTIVALS

C. J. Jackson

Illustrated by Annie Starkey

HarperCollins*Publishers*

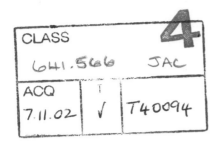
HarperCollins*Publishers*
77–85 Fulham Palace Road, London W6 8JB
www.**fire**and**water**.com

First published in Great Britain in 2001 by HarperCollins*Publishers*

1 3 5 7 9 10 8 6 4 2

A catalogue record for this book is available from the British Library.

ISBN 0 00 711960 7

Printed and bound in Great Britain by
Bath Press Ltd

FOR ROD
– especially the chocolate recipes

CONTENTS

WINTER FEASTS

SPRING FEASTS

SUMMER FEASTS

AUTUMN FEASTS

CONVERSIONS AND ABBREVIATIONS

The recipes are written in metric, imperial and American cup measurements.

When you are cooking a recipe, use whichever type of measurement you prefer, but don't combine them.

American cup measures are available from some cookery shops outside the USA.
One American cup = 250ml (8fl.oz), which is ½ US pint.

Tablespoon measures in Europe and the USA are the same.

ABBREVIATIONS
tbsp = tablespoon
tsp = teaspoon
ltr = litre

All tablespoon or teaspoon measures are level, unless specified otherwise.

There is a time for everything and a season for every activity under heaven: a time to be born and a time to die, a time to plant and a time to uproot, a time to kill and a time to heal, a time to tear down and a time to build, a time to weep and a time to laugh, a time to mourn and a time to dance, a time to scatter stones and a time to gather them, a time to embrace and a time to refrain, a time to search and a time to give up, a time to keep and a time to throw away, a time to tear and a time to mend, a time to be silent and a time to speak, a time to love and a time to hate, a time for war and a time for peace.

Ecclesiastes 3:1–8 (New International Version)

FOREWORD
by Marguerite Patten O.B.E.

Reading any comprehensive calendar, almanac or diary, you may be surprised to see just how many special days and festivals there are in the year. Easter and Christmas are widely celebrated but most of the others can be over-looked. In this interesting and unusual book C. J. Jackson gives the reader lots of wonderful excuses to revive the importance of these dates as social and family occasions. Throughout the book helpful religious and historical facts are followed by original, exciting and practical recipes for a range of dishes to make each a memorable event.

Looking through the extensive range of meals I was struck by the clever choice of recipes. The Feast Days of Great Britain's Saints are celebrated in style: splendid shellfish and lamb recipes form the basis for the Welsh dishes of St David's Day, while on St George's Day one would feast on beef, cooked in a new way, and follow this with a sumptuous syllabub and a savoury based on English cheeses. The dishes suggested for St Patrick's and St Andrew's Days are equally tempting. Meanwhile the recipe for St Valentine's Day is suitably enticing!

Each season of the year is covered in turn, so under Winter we begin by being reminded of an old tradition, in Stir Up Sunday, when the initial preparations for Christmas begin. This is followed by Advent, where one finds memorable information on this important religious period, along with recipes that will delight friends and family alike, and clever ideas for edible gifts. The dishes for Christmas and the New Year are unusual and exciting.

The rest of the year is covered with equal skill. Spring includes Lenten dishes, a delicious tea-time menu for Mothering Sunday and delightful menus for the Easter festival. In Summer there are recipes for Whitsun and those once-in-a-lifetime occasions like a family wedding or a Christening.

With this book you will never be at a loss about cooking a special meal for a special occasion. In addition, I am sure you will gain enormously from the extra information on the importance of our various Feasts and Festivals and the richness this brings to our celebration of them.

ACKNOWLEDGEMENTS

Most books in publication would not be possible without a huge support cast. This recipe book is no exception.

A large number of friends and colleagues ate their way through many of the feasts in this book; I am really appreciative of the comments and suggestions rendered.

My sincere thanks go particularly to the team at the HarperCollins *Religious* department, especially the commissioning editor, Amy Boucher Pye, who along with Jeremy Yates-Round and Elspeth Taylor gave me the opportunity to create this book and create and celebrate all the feasts in it.

Thanks also to the cookery editor, Clare Atkins, and my close friend and illustrator, Annie Starkey, who in essence has given life to my recipes and food; and to Cindy Marie Harvey, my travelling companion, who provided the wine suggestions.

It is usually unwise for the creator of a recipe to actually test it for reliability and accuracy, so a team of brilliant home economists have painstakingly worked their way through the menus; they include Becca Ford, Lori Poulton, and Sandra Purkess.

Special thanks too to Sarah Pawson, Sally Morris, Liz Capper, Don and Joan Ashworth, who all gave me masses of encouragement and their own thoughts about feasts.

And finally, this book gave me time to reflect about families too. I realized how parents in particular are a great source of support – perhaps it is time to create a 'Parents' Feast Day'. My mum, Ann, was constantly supplying me with plenty of seasonal produce, biblical references and enthusiasm and, of course, my dad who had lots of ideas and was always there when he was needed.

THOUGHTS ON FEASTING
AND HOW TO USE THIS BOOK

WHY THE BOOK?

Sunday was an important family day during my childhood. It was the one day of the week that we would all share a meal together, usually roast lamb or beef, followed by a very 'English' pudding!

With the distractions of the twenty-first century, the changes in family life and the speed with which we lead our lives, the opportunity to sit around the table and enjoy a meal is harder to achieve, especially in the home. With the tearing rush to compete with time, the months and years seem to flash past faster and faster, the seasons seem to merge and are gone. Christmas, Easter and days such as St Valentine's and Whitsun present an opportunity to gather friends and family together to celebrate everything that we have, and perhaps a time to reflect on the history upon which they are based.

Although I have taught and written about food for many years I still love to cook for friends and family, particularly Sunday lunch. These occasions are for me a time to relax, enjoy companionship and indulge in good food. Preparing and cooking a meal, however simple, is all about a shared experience – an essential time for communicating, giving, talking and laughing. Time to catch up with old friends and meet new. A celebration of life and our humanity.

WHAT FEASTS AND FESTIVALS?

The book focuses on many well-known feasts and some that may have been forgotten, but also on the day-to-day family occasions that we all come together to celebrate: christenings, weddings, anniversaries, birthdays and Thanksgiving.

Each festival, wherever you are in the world, brings with it a host of traditional, time-honoured ingredients and recipes that are still used today. Think of Christmas in a cold climate and immediately thoughts of mince pies, roast turkey or a glazed ham come to mind. The menus that I have compiled for each occasion will have a familiar ring, but each is given its own little twist.

ABOUT FEAST DAYS AND FESTIVALS

Sunday was set aside as a day of rest; it is the first day of the week and the pivotal day on which our calendar is based. The early Christian Church kept a Sabbath day and celebrated the resurrection of Christ at Easter, his Ascension and the day of the Pentecost. It was only after the recognition of the Christian Church by the Romans in the fourth century that other feast days began to play a part in the calendar. Celebrations of Christ's birthday at Christmas and all the many other saints' days have evolved over the last two thousand years.

Before the Christian calendar became established there were many seasonal rituals that were dictated by the sun. In the spring and autumn there are the two equinoxes, days where hours of dark and light are equal. The winter and summer solstices are the days in December and June when the sun is respectively at its weakest and strongest. These festivals based upon the movements of the sun were included in the Christian calendar to illustrate the life and work of Christ.

The birth of Christ is celebrated just after the pre-Christian winter solstice and demonstrates the bringing of illuminating light to the world as the sun begins to grow strong again. Easter is celebrated soon after the spring equinox when new life is being created. It is timed to coincide with the Jewish Passover, this being the time that Christ was crucified according to Scripture. The feast of Passover is always held about the time of the first full moon after the spring equinox. The celebration of Christ's life is played out during the year along with the festivals associated with saints.

The Jewish calendar was established thousands of years ago and it is steeped in traditions and rituals. Many celebrations take place as part of the Jewish year. Like the Christian church calendar, cooking for Jews revolves around the Sabbath and other festivals and feast days. For Jews the Sabbath is a very special day, one of joy. Food prepared for this day is always good – the best, no expense to be spared – in comparison to the simple diet of the week.

The Sabbath is not only celebrated with food, but the table is laid with the best cloth, silver and china. The Sabbath and all the feasts and festivals of the Jews are an essential and very important part of family life and that of the community. They adhere to the fourth Commandment: 'six days shall they labour'.

Food plays an important role in many feasts and festivals. Where Christian diet is varied, the role of food for Jews is symbolic and relates closely to the day of celebration. It is often mentioned in the Torah, the holy book containing the Ten Commandments. Just as the celebrations of the Christian year are dictated mainly by the sun, the movements of the moon dictate the Jewish calendar.

MOVEABLE FEASTS

Although there are many set feast days each year, Easter is decided by the date of Passover and so there are several moveable feasts, never celebrated on the same day. Ascension Day comes forty days after Easter and Pentecost or Whitsun is fifty days or seven weeks after Easter.

The first day of the week, Sunday, is of particular importance, designated as a day of rest. The early Christians would celebrate each Sunday as if it was Easter Day. The two other particularly important days for the church are Wednesday and Friday, which are a reminder of Christ's sacrifice. Wednesday was the day that Judas betrayed Christ – it became a day of penitence and fasting. The bleakest day of the Christian calendar, Good Friday, is remembered weekly and in some parts of the world, fish is still served on that day.

COOKING WITH THE SEASONS

I particularly enjoy cooking with the produce, fruit and vegetables that each season brings. Even though not all the ingredients I enjoy to cook may be available on my own doorstep, many fruits and vegetables, imported from around the world and available in the supermarkets, also have their own season. I use these at a time when homegrown produce is a little scarce. So with each feast, I have with a few exceptions used seasonal produce.

The book is roughly divided into the four seasons: not precisely by month, but by a balance of celebrations. A large majority of well-known festivals and feasts are in the winter and spring months. So I have taken the opportunity to create a chapter for family celebrations during the summer, when church life has moved into a quieter time. Throughout the church calendar there are dozens of saints' days, too many to include – in the end I chose a handful to celebrate.

A LITTLE ABOUT THE HISTORY

The history behind the celebrations and traditions of feast days gives us some understanding of how each became established. When life ran at a slower, steadier pace and times were hard, feasts and festivals played an important role for the Church and the home. Even before the Church became established there were many pagan rituals which followed the pattern of the seasons. These traditions eventually became encompassed by the Church to form the calendar of events and feast days as we know them today. I have based many of my recipes on ingredients that have been passed down through the centuries.

HOW TO USE THIS BOOK

Although seasonal, with the wide availability of ingredients today most of the menus can be re-created at any time of the year.

The Index is important – When you look through this book, take time to look at the Index, as you will find a host of recipes. Christmas for many in the UK would not be complete without a roast turkey – there is a great recipe, but it is included as part of the Thanksgiving celebration. If you prefer a goose, you will find that served at the feast of St Michael or Michaelmas, at the end of September.

Recipes and menus – The menus on the whole are a celebration and I hope that the recipes create just that feeling. The reflective time of Lent, when the early Church forbade the eating of meat and dairy products, made me think about healthier recipes and several of the menus have been put together with that in mind.

The beginning of each chapter – You will find a summary here about the feasts celebrated during each season. Not all have been included along with a menu; there would be far too many to contemplate. To introduce each individual feast day or celebration there is a brief introduction explaining the religious context, some historical detail if applicable and a note about the seasonal ingredients.

About the recipe quantities – Each feast day menu has a note as to how many people each recipe will feed. This may seem a little daunting at first, as larger quantities can be a little frightening if you are used to cooking for small numbers. But it seems pointless to give a recipe for a Christmas dinner that will only feed four, when many people have to cook for a larger number. An afternoon wedding tea will invariably be for a larger number, whereas the festival of St Valentine is an intimate occasion and the recipes will serve two. If you do need to reduce or increase the amount of ingredients, take a look at the conversion chart which is included as part of 'Planning a Feast' (see below); this should help.

Eat and enjoy – Lastly, this book is all about celebration, so I hope you will cook, eat and particularly enjoy.

$\mathcal{P}$LANNING A FEAST

Some things to remember about planning a party.

Don't feel it is essential to cook a complete menu as written, pick and choose as you see fit. Remember that no recipe or menu is a final destination, it is a point from which to start – so adapt and add to or subtract from each recipe, as you wish.

I am a firm believer in ease and speed in cooking. I have tried to use only ingredients that I know to be readily available in the supermarket, although you may find one or two things are not easy to come by. Under these circumstances I have tried to give an alternative ingredient to use in its place, so again, be flexible.

All the recipes have been tested for reliability and quantities but one can never be absolutely exact. The cooking times for any recipe will vary from one oven and stove to another, and appetites also differ, so be instinctive when you are buying, preparing and cooking food.

The recipes are designed to celebrate food and feast days, and I hope this is reflected in the recipes. The combination of recipes for each of the feast days does not always constitute a complete menu. In many cases the menu will need to be balanced by the addition of a selection of vegetables, a salad or carbohydrate: potatoes, rice or pasta. Just remember to think about colour combinations and make sure each menu has a good balance of textures.

Although some of the menus are for larger numbers, it is always unwise to plan a big party and use unfamiliar recipes unless you are a really confident cook. Try things out as you go, or before a big event, so that you feel confident. It is important if you are cooking for a feast that you too enjoy the celebrations.

AMERICAN GLOSSARY OF INGREDIENTS

Dry goods

Plain flour = all-purpose flour
    A soft flour, perfect for pastry and
    cake making
Self-raising flour = self-rising flour
    Soft flour with a raising agent, used in
    some cakes
Strong plain flour = bread flour
    A high gluten 'strong' flour, suitable
    for bread making
Cornflour = cornstarch
    A gluten-free thickening agent, used
    for sauces
Bicarbonate of soda = baking soda
Icing sugar = confectioner's/
    powdered sugar
    Very fine ground sugar, used for some
    icings and to give a sweet dusting
Caster sugar = superfine sugar
    Fine sugar, used for cakes
Granulated sugar = sugar
    Coarse crystal sugar, used for caramels
    and syrups
Muscovado/light/dark brown sugar =
    brown sugar
    The texture, size and shapes of brown
    sugar crystals vary from type to type
Demerara sugar = turbinado sugar
    Course-crystal golden brown sugar,
    often used for coffee

Dairy

It's worth checking the fat quantity of
creams or dairy produce – anything with a
fat quantity of less than 30% will not whip
effectively and will separate if boiled too
vigorously.
Double cream = heavy whipping or
    thick cream
Whipping cream = light whipping cream
Single cream = light or coffee cream
Crème fraîche is difficult to find in some
parts of the USA – it's a lightly soured
cream, usually with a fat proportion of over
38%. In the absence of this, you can use
double cream, mixed with a little Greek
yoghurt.

Fromage frais is a fresh white cheese of a
pouring consistency. The fat content varies,
but is usually about 15–18% butter fat.
Again, this can be difficult to source in the
US; Greek yoghurt is a good substitute.

Vegetables etc.

Spring onions = green, scallion or
    salad onions
Rocket = arugula
Coriander = cilantro
Courgettes = zucchini
Aubergine = eggplant
Hazelnuts = filbert nuts
Tomato purée = tomato paste
Florentine fennel = fennel bulb

Baking utensils

Bun tin = patty tin
Swiss roll tin = jelly roll pan
Spring-form tin = spring-form pan

QUICK REFERENCE TO ANNUAL FEASTS AND FESTIVALS

Dates are moveable according to the sacred calendar, unless stated.

January	New Year's Day (1st)
	Twelfth Night (5th)
	and Epiphany (6th)
	Burns Night (25th)
	Australia Day (26th)
February	Candlemas (2nd)
	St Valentine's Day (14th)
	Shrove Tuesday
	(precedes Ash Wednesday)
	Ash Wednesday
	(beginning of Lent)
March	St David's Day (1st)
	Commonwealth Day (11th)
	St Patrick's Day (17th)
	Vernal (Spring) Equinox (21st)
	Mothering Sunday
April	Holy Week
	Jewish Passover
	Palm Sunday
	(precedes Easter Sunday)
	Maundy Thursday
	(precedes Good Friday)
	Good Friday
	Easter Sunday
	St George's Day (23rd)
May	May Day (1st)
	Ascension Day
	(40 days after Easter)

Jewish Pentecost/Whitsun
(50 days after Easter)

June	Trinity Sunday
	Father's Day
	Midsummer's Day (21st)
	(US: The longest day)
July	American Independence Day (4th)
	St Swithun's Day (15th)
August	Lammas (1st)
	St Bartholomew's Day (24th)
September	Birth of Mary, Mother of Jesus (8th)
	Rosh Hashanah (Jewish New Year)
	Yom Kippur
	Autumnal Equinox (23rd)
	Michaelmas (29th)
October	Sukkoth (Feast of Tabernacles)
	All Hallows' Eve (31st)
November	All Saints' Day (1st)
	All Souls' Day (2nd)
	Martinmas (11th)
	Remembrance Day (11th)
	American Thanksgiving (the fourth Thursday)
	St Andrew's Day (30th)
December	Stir-up Sunday (Sunday before Advent)

Advent (four Sundays)
Feast of St Nicholas (6th)
Feast of St Lucia (13th)
Hanukah
Christmas Eve (24th)
Christmas Day (25th)
St Stephen's Day
(GB: Boxing Day) (26th)
New Year's Eve (31st)

Winter Feasts

*T*hrough the centuries, from before the birth of Christ, to the establishment of the early Church until the present day, the cold, dark days of winter have always been the time for people to come together and celebrate the many feasts that the season brings. The feasts that we still celebrate today have been an important part of our heritage over hundreds of years.

Yet many of the original reasons for celebration have been forgotten with the passage of time. Wonderful as it is, much of our fresh produce is available all year round and this choice has taken away some of the excitement of enjoying each food in its own season. Climate change over the years means that these days we often have a warm or wet spell in October, and autumn seems to linger well into November. Nevertheless by December the leaves have gone from the trees, the days are very short, the evenings long and the cold weather has well and truly set in. Winter is here. Our ancestors, without the many conveniences and luxuries of today's lifestyle, would have been preparing for the onset of the cold months during autumn.

Although it falls on 11 November, the feast of St Martin (Martinmas) was at one time officially the first day of winter. To the early Christians 11 November was also the beginning of Advent. Today we realize that winter is upon us only sometime in mid December, when the temperature is dropping outside and temperatures are rising inside with the overwhelming bustle of a commercial Christmas just around the corner.

The Christmas cycle is the official start of the Church year, beginning around All Souls' Day, late October to early November. This period holds several preparation Sundays leading to the four Sundays in Advent, which in December prepare us for the Christmas celebrations on the 25th and the following days.

Our midwinter feasts begin on the Sunday immediately before Advent. History relates that this day was known as Stir-up Sunday, or Stirring-up Sunday. It was the day when the cooking began for Christmas, with the whole family joining in to make a Christmas pudding.

Then we move into Advent itself. Although an exciting time to make ready for celebrating the birth of Christ, Advent was at one time a period of fasting. Commercially this is considered the most important feasting and family time of the year, although to the Church the celebration of Easter is more meaningful.

There is an Advent tradition of placing in churches a wreath holding five candles; one is lit on each of the four Sundays in Advent and they represent peace, joy, hope and love. The fifth candle, in the centre, is lit on Christmas Day and represents Christ.

6 December is the feast day of St Nicholas, the figure on whom the jolly bringer of gifts, Father Christmas or Santa Claus, is based. St Nicholas was a bishop during the fourth century and history relates that he gave children gifts on this day; it is this giving that gave rise to the tradition of presents on 25 December. In times past it was this day that was celebrated as Christmas, the day when the gift of Christ was made to the world.

The feast of St Lucia is celebrated on 13 December, exactly twelve days before Christmas, and is an important feast day particularly in Scandinavia and Hungary. The saint was a young girl who was martyred in the fourth century for her miraculous works. The day is also called the Festival of Light.

Hanukah – the Jewish festival of light – is celebrated over eight days and usually falls sometime in December. It is a time to commemorate the victory of an army of Jews fighting under the leadership of Judas Maccabeus. They returned to Jerusalem after their victory only to discover that the temple had been desecrated. Only a little of the holy consecrated oil was untouched. The tiny amount of oil remaining was considered enough to last only for a day or so, yet it miraculously lasted for eight days while the priests cleansed the temple and prepared

new oil. As with many Jewish festivals, the foods traditionally served at Hanukah are symbolic: deep-fried dishes are particularly popular at this time, as is goose, a custom adopted by the Christian Church for the celebration of Christmas.

The excitement of the Christmas preparations during Advent culminates on Christmas Eve. Christ's birth is celebrated at midnight on 24 December, with a communion service. Christmas Day is a day for rejoicing at the birth of the infant Jesus. Over the centuries many traditional foods and recipes have been created for the Christmas period, all based on produce that was available at that time of year. Today there are so many traditions attached to Christmas that it is easy to forget the simplicity behind the occasion.

Carol singing to celebrate the birth of Christ was well established by the sixteenth century; it was only in the puritanical times during the seventeenth century that these celebrations where banned and Christmas Day was considered a normal working day. Penalties for taking part in any form of celebrations, including the singing of carols, were severe. Many Christians were determined to keep to their traditional practices and it was during this time that the carol 'The Twelve Days of Christmas' became popular, as it held a hidden meaning for Christian believers. Each gift on the twelve days held a different biblical or spiritual meaning: 'my true love' represented God, the 'partridge in a pear tree' Christ and so forth.

Boxing Day, or the feast of St Stephen, falls on 26 December. The feast of the Holy Innocents is remembered by the Church on 28 December; it commemorates the massacre of all male children under two years old ordered by Herod in his attempts to end the life of the infant Christ.

New Year is a celebration dating back to pagan rituals. In Scotland, where it is known as Hogmanay, it is a festival of great importance. The twelve days of Christmas traditionally ended with a feast on Twelfth Night, 5 January. Epiphany on 6 January commemorates the day that the three kings visited the infant Jesus; some cultures, particularly in the Mediterranean, celebrate this day instead of 25 December with the giving of gifts and, of course, a feast.

The Monday following Epiphany was at one time known as Plough Monday. This was the day that winter ploughing began in earnest, ready for planting crops when the weather began to warm. Ashes from the burnt Yule log would be sprinkled across the ploughed land and a priest's blessing would be made to ensure a good yield of crops that year.

Through the cold and rather dreary month of January other saints' days are celebrated, as is custom in the Catholic Church, but the birthday of the famous Scottish poet, Robert Burns, on 25 January is a particularly important event in the Scottish calendar. Burns Night fare traditionally includes haggis accompanied by drams of whisky; the meal is followed by readings of Burns's poetry.

Catholic communities celebrate Candlemas on 2 February. It commemorates the day that Mary took the infant Jesus to the temple for dedication. It is also the day that the white church candles used throughout the year are consecrated, and it brings the first thoughts of spring, light and hopes for the year ahead. The feast of St Valentine, patron saint of lovers, celebrated on 14 February is another commercial opportunity for many and another day of feasting. The end of the Christmas cycle for the Church leads into the important cycle of Lent and the spring.

SEASONAL INGREDIENTS IN WINTER

The colder weather brings with it the need for warming foods and the earth's natural cycle yields many foods to fulfil that need. The further north you live, the harder life is and the less produce is available.

Many root vegetables are available, including parsnips, turnips, celeriac, swede and beetroot. Maincrop potatoes are harvested earlier in the year; as they do not like frost they will not survive through the winter. Most varieties, however, store well during the long winter months and are an essential standby. Varieties of potato that are particularly good include King Edward and Maris Piper.

Greens that flourish in the winter include members of the brassica family, such as cabbages: red, Dutch and Savoy are all great at this time. Cauliflowers, kohlrabi and, of course, Brussels sprouts are all in their prime.

Some lettuces survive under cloches during the winter, including hearted varieties such as Iceberg and Webb's Wonder. All of the bitter chicory family are in season, along with the hardy lamb's lettuce. If grown in a protected area, spinach and rocket are also available.

The alliums (onion family) are in plentiful supply. Leeks weather the winter well, although the delicate chives and spring onions do not reappear until the ground begins to warm. Stores of onions and garlic from the summer months will keep through the year. The traditional day to plant the new year's crop of onion and garlic sets is at the shortest day of the year in December. This gives the alliums a long period under the soil in which to become established.

The wild game season is in full swing by December and it is perhaps no coincidence that in bygone years domestic animals were scarce at this time. There was little to feed stock on during the winter months and therefore only the essential beasts would be weathered and kept through the winter. Meat was salted or dried to help ensure a supply of food. Only the landowners or the wealthy were allowed to shoot or pay for game: needless to say, poaching was rife!

Today many types of game, including pheasant, partridge, hare, wild boar and venison, are in plentiful supply for the table. The grouse season, which is the first to begin in August, is also the first to finish on 10 December.

Although many orchard fruits store well through the winter months, softer fruits are not plentiful at this time. Homegrown apple varieties are particularly good, the perfect stocking filler and eating apple for Christmas being the Cox's Orange Pippin. Produce from warmer climes comes into its own. Pomegranates, cranberries, grapes, lychees, physalis (Cape gooseberries) and persimmons are plentiful and are therefore often included as a traditional part of the festivities. Exotic fruits from tropical climates are also in plentiful supply, including bananas, mangoes, pineapples and of course dates.

Citrus fruits also come into their own: many varieties of the loose-skinned mandarin family are in good supply. Other stocking fillers which make good eating at this time are clementines, satsumas and tangerines. The sour Seville orange, which is used for marmalade making, is in season for a few short weeks in January – so this is the time for making marmalade for the year ahead.

Whatever your celebration or family occasion, enjoy feasting during the cold winter months.

Three-chocolate Yuletide Log

The old English name of Yule refers to a long-forgotten Anglo-Saxon festival held at the winter solstice. It has been adopted now to be part of our modern Christmas celebrations.

SERVES 8–10

340g (12oz/1½ cups) dark chocolate (minimum 70% cocoa solids)

55g (2oz/¼ cup) unsalted butter

3 tbsp rum

4 tbsp cold strong coffee

3 tbsp ground rice

6 eggs, separated

110g (4oz/½ cup) caster sugar

200g (7oz/⅞ cup) milk chocolate, roughly chopped

3 tbsp single cream

225g (8oz/1 cup) unsalted butter

85g (3oz/⅜ cup) caster sugar

Grated zest of 1 orange

110g (4oz/½ cup) white chocolate, finely chopped

Icing sugar, to decorate

Heat the oven to 190ºC (375ºF/gas mark 5). Line a large baking tray 35–40cm (14–16in) x 22–25cm (9–10in) with a double layer of non-stick baking parchment, folding it at the corners to form a case. Secure the corners with paper clips.

Put the chocolate, butter, rum and coffee into a saucepan and stir over a very low heat, until the butter has liquefied and the chocolate has nearly melted. Remove it from the heat, stir in the ground rice and leave it to cool.

Put the egg whites into a clean glass bowl. Whisk until a stiff peak forms. Add the sugar, a little at a time, whisking well between each addition. Fold the egg whites and egg yolks into the chocolate sauce. Spoon the mixture into the prepared paper case and bake on the middle shelf of the oven for 18–20 minutes or until the mixture has set and a heavy sugary crust has formed. Slide the cooked roulade on to a wire rack and leave to cool in the paper case covered with a sheet of dampened greaseproof paper for at least 1 hour.

For the filling, melt the milk chocolate together with the cream, in a bowl set over a saucepan of simmering water, then leave to cool. Beat the butter, sugar and orange zest until creamy, fold the mixture into the melted chocolate and stir in the white chocolate.

To assemble the log, turn the cold roulade upside down on to a piece of greaseproof paper which has been lightly dusted with icing sugar. Pull away the paper casing from the bottom and sides, and trim the edges of the roulade to neaten. Spread one-third of the chocolate filling over the roulade, then roll it up, starting from a long side, into a log shape. Spread the remaining chocolate filling over the top and sides and use a fork or palette knife to score lines on the surface.

Dust the Yuletide Log with icing sugar and serve.

STIR-UP SUNDAY

At one time, the Sunday immediately before Advent was a special family day when the preparations for Christmas began. It became known as 'Stir-up Sunday' as this was the day for making traditional Christmas pudding. The whole family was involved in this special occasion – each member would have the opportunity to stir the pudding and wish for a secret blessing.

Trinkets, each with its own meaning, such as a wedding ring, thimble, horseshoe or button, and some money, would be added to the pudding, to be retrieved when it was served. Little silver tokens can still be bought today, but remember to tell your guests if they are included.

Plum pudding, which is now synonymous with Christmas, was at one time served at most family celebrations and feasts, including Lent. The word 'plum' was used to describe many types of dried fruit. The original pudding is thought to have been a pottage (thick broth), made with stewed meat. Over the years, the recipe evolved until all the meat, with the exception of suet, was replaced with fruit. The whole mixture was wrapped and boiled in a cloth.

Traditional rich-boiled Christmas puddings mature extremely well and are often best stored for a year. The recipe provided here will give you at least three puddings – enough to store until next year if you can.

Old-fashioned Boiled Plum Pudding

MAKES 3 X 1LTR (1¾ PINT) PUDDINGS

340g (12oz/5½ cups) wholemeal breadcrumbs

225g (8oz/1½ cups) prunes, stoned and chopped

340g (12oz/3 cups) dates, stoned and chopped

Thoroughly mix all the ingredients together in a large bowl. Divide the mixture between three 1ltr (1¾ pint) pudding basins each lined with a double layer of muslin. Tie the muslin around the pudding and cover the top of each basin with a double layer of non-stick baking parchment and aluminium foil. Tie the corners on tightly with string and trim away any excess paper and foil.

340g (12oz/4½ cups) currants

340g (12oz/2 heaped cups) sultanas or raisins

225g (8oz/1½ cups) dried figs, chopped

225g (8oz/2 cups) fresh suet, grated

225g (8oz/2 cups) self-raising flour

110g (4oz/⅔ cup) candied citrus peel, chopped (see recipe on page 51)

55g (2oz/½ cup) blanched almonds, roughly chopped

1 tsp mixed spice

1 tsp freshly grated nutmeg

½ tsp ground cinnamon

1 tsp salt

6 eggs, beaten

Lower each pudding into a large saucepan half-filled with boiling water. Boil the puddings for 6 hours. Keep the water level topped up with fresh boiling water, but avoid pouring it over the top of the covered puddings.

The puddings can be made well in advance. To reheat them for serving, remove the original paper and foil tops and replace them with new covers. Boil the puddings for at least 1½ hours, then serve with Rum, Orange and Coconut Butter (see page 45).

Traditional Rich Fruit Cake

This fruit cake is not only perfect for Christmas, but is also the ideal base for traditional wedding or formal occasion cakes.

Ideally, make this at least 3 weeks before eating. Feed it with a little brandy during this time, but don't overdo it, or the cake will become too soggy and will crumble when decorated.

FOR A 25CM (9IN) CAKE

500g (1lb 2oz/2$^{1}/_{2}$ cups) bag mixed dried fruits (currants, sultanas, raisins and mixed peel)

225g (8oz/1$^{1}/_{2}$ cups) semi-dried figs, chopped

225g (8oz/1$^{1}/_{2}$ cups) semi-dried prunes, pitted and chopped

4 tbsp rum or brandy

2 tbsp black treacle

110g (4oz/$^{2}/_{3}$ cup) mixed coloured glacé cherries, halved

55g (2oz/$^{1}/_{2}$ cup) unblanched Brazil nuts or almonds, chopped

Grated zest of 1 lemon

250g (9oz/1$^{1}/_{8}$ cups) plain flour

1 tsp ground ginger

$^{1}/_{8}$ tsp freshly grated nutmeg
1 tsp mixed spice

55g (2oz/$^{1}/_{2}$ cup) ground almonds

170g (6oz/$^{3}/_{4}$ cup) butter or margarine

170g (6oz/1 cup) dark muscovado sugar

5 eggs, beaten

The day before you plan to make the cake, put the prepared dried fruits into a large plastic bag, pour over the rum and add the treacle. Shake the bag well and leave it to soak for 24 hours. The next day, add the cherries, Brazil nuts and lemon zest.

To prepare the cake tin, lightly oil a 25cm (10in) deep cake tin. Line the sides of the tin with two layers of non-stick baking parchment – take a long strip, fold it in half lengthways, then fold up 2.5cm (1in) along one long edge and snip into this narrow fold at intervals to allow the paper to bend around the base of the tin. Then cut a single disc of paper the size of the tin and use it to line the base. Tie a sheet of brown paper or newspaper around the outside of the tin.

Heat the oven to 140°C (275°F/gas mark 1).

Sift the flour and spices together and add the ground almonds. Cream the butter and sugar together until very light and fluffy. Add the eggs, a splash at a time, and beat well between each addition. If the mixture curdles, add a spoonful of the flour mixture.

Add the flour and soaked fruits to the creamed mixture and stir until well combined. Spoon the cake mixture into the prepared tin, pushing it up the sides of the tin a little to make a slight indentation in the centre of the cake – this will help to give the cake a flat top.

Cover a baking sheet with a 1cm ($^{1}/_{2}$in) layer of salt and sit the cake tin on top. Bake in the centre of the oven for 2$^{1}/_{2}$–3 hours, or until a skewer inserted into the centre comes out clean. Cover the top with aluminium foil if the cake begins to darken.

Once the cake is cooked, remove it from the oven and leave it to cool completely in the tin. Remove it, leaving the baking parchment around it until you are ready to decorate it.

CHRISTMAS CAKE DECORATION

Everyone has their own way of decorating a Christmas cake. If you have children, it is fun to do this with them just before Christmas. If you are in a hurry, a selection of dried fruits or seasonal fresh fruits arranged on top is a really effective and quick way to finish the cake, while marzipan and fondant or royal icing is traditional and allows you to add any Christmas figures and decorations you may have. The quantities needed for this fruit cake are as follows:

Dried fruit topping

You will need:

340g–450g (^{3}/4–1lb/1^1/2–2 cups) dried fruit and nuts, such as apricots, Brazil nuts, dried figs and dates

You can include a selection of fresh fruits, such as physalis, stoned medjool dates and sliced kumquats – look around the shelves of your grocer and see what appeals to you. Arrange the prepared fruit on top of the cake and brush the whole with warm apricot jam mixed with a splash or two of rum.

Marzipan and fondant icing

You will need:

225g (8oz/1 cup) quantity for top of the cake only

675g (1^1/2 lb/3 cups) quantity for top and sides

When using marzipan and fondant icing, remember to brush the cake with warm apricot jam before putting the marzipan on.

ADVENT

Advent – meaning 'coming forward' – is a hopeful time. The early Church began its celebrations forty days before Christmas, which fell on the same day as the first day of the old Celtic winter. Advent was eventually shortened to four weeks – it now starts on the fourth Sunday before Christmas – as it was considered a less important time than Lent (also forty days), which leads up to Easter Sunday. At one time, Advent was also a time of penitence and fasting, and although this aspect of the tradition has died out, it's still a time of preparation for the celebration of Jesus' birth. It's not only a busy period for the Church, but also a time for entertaining family and friends, culminating in the festivities of Christmas Day.

The recipe and menu suggestions below should be helpful if you're entertaining during Advent, and are followed by a selection to help you plan if you'd like to cook ahead for Christmas.

ENTERTAINING IN ADVENT

ADVENT TEA

Chestnut and Chocolate Truffle Cake

Savoury toasted sandwiches or buttered crumpets with Gentleman's Relish, followed by this special cake, will make a memorable Advent tea.

FINGER FOOD FOR AN ADVENT DRINKS PARTY

Marinated Herb Chicken
and Bacon Kebabs
Wild Boar Sausage and Chestnut
Tortilla Wraps
Baked Winter Vegetable Wedges
with Garlic Mayonnaise
Potted Red Leicester Cheese with
Toasted Hazelnuts
Lime Chilli Prawns
Mini Apple and Mincemeat
Strudels
Macadamia Meringue Kisses

Drinks parties are a great way to entertain a large group of friends all at once. Food for these occasions can be informal, but it has to be satisfying, too. These ideas can all be prepared or cooked in advance, so you can enjoy being with your guests. Each recipe will feed in excess of thirty people – for a pre-dinner drinks party, one of each recipe is enough, but if you aim to feed people throughout the evening, make sure you have a minimum of fifteen bites per person.

A simple and appealing Australian Chardonnay and a classic Mulled Wine (see page 41) are both ideal for a pre-Christmas drinks party.

PLANNING AHEAD FOR CHRISTMAS

RECIPES FOR THE CHRISTMAS SEASON

Satsuma and Cinnamon
    Marmalade
Fruit Mincemeat
Marzipan Mince Pies
Rum, Orange and Coconut Butter
Cranberry and Port Relish
Christmas Stollen
Chestnut, Chocolate and
    Mincemeat Semi-freddo Pudding

All of the above can be prepared in advance and either frozen or refrigerated

CHRISTMAS TREATS OR GIFTS

After-dinner petits fours:
Three-chocolate Truffles
Caramel Spiced Nuts
Candied Citrus Peel
Mini Ginger Melting Moments

If you have any room for them, a tray of petits fours is a festive and colourful way to conclude the Christmas meal. Serve them with coffee and Frosted Fruit (see page 65). A selection of gift-wrapped, hand-made petits fours also makes a delightful Christmas present.

Chestnut and Chocolate Truffle Cake

Frosted Fruit (see page 65) arranged around this cake will give a festive finish.

SERVES 6

110g (4oz/^{1}/$_2$ cup) cooked chestnuts

4 large eggs

140g (5oz/^{5}/$_8$ cup) caster sugar

85g (3oz/^{5}/$_8$ cup) plain flour

^{1}/$_2$ tsp baking powder
55g (2oz/^{1}/$_4$ cup) butter, melted

1 tbsp rum

For the frosting:

200g (7oz/^{7}/$_8$ cup) dark chocolate (minimum 70% cocoa solids)

140g (5oz/1^1/$_4$ cups) crème fraîche

1 tsp strong black coffee

2–3 tbsp caster sugar

10 Three-chocolate Truffles (see page 49), to decorate (optional)

Grind the chestnuts to a powder in a food processor and set aside. Heat the oven to 180ºC (350ºF/gas mark 4).

Separate the eggs. Place the yolks in a bowl with 110g (4oz) of the caster sugar and whisk until light and fluffy. Place the whites in a clean glass bowl and whisk until very stiff, then add the remaining caster sugar, a teaspoonful at a time, until the mixture is very shiny and glossy.

Sift the flour and baking powder into the yolk mixture, then add the whisked egg whites, melted butter, chestnuts and rum. Fold gently until all the ingredients are just incorporated. Pour the meringue into a well-greased 20cm (8in) spring-form mould.

Bake in the centre of the oven for 25–35min, or until the cake has risen and will spring back to the touch. Remove it from the oven and leave to cool in the tin for 15min before turning it on to a wire rack to cool completely.

To make the frosting, chop up the chocolate and put it into a glass bowl set over a saucepan of simmering water (don't let the water touch the bowl). Stir until the chocolate has just begun to melt, remove it from the heat and allow it to melt completely. Put aside to cool for 5min.

Stir the crème fraîche, coffee and sugar together, then fold this into the cooled, but still runny, chocolate.

Cut the cake to make two layers and spread half of the frosting over the bottom layer. Sandwich the cake halves together and spread the remaining frosting on top. Arrange the truffles on the frosting (if using), and serve.

Marinated Herb Chicken and Bacon Kebabs

MAKES 36

4 chicken breasts, skin removed

3 tbsp olive oil

1 tbsp finely chopped sage

1 tbsp finely chopped rosemary

10 rashers streaky bacon

A little wholegrain mustard

For the dipping sauce:

250ml (8fl oz/1 cup) soured cream

1 tsp tomato purée

Dijon mustard, to taste

2 spring onions, finely chopped

36 bamboo skewers, each 12.5cm (5in) long, soaked in hot water for 30min

Sprigs of sage or rosemary, to serve

Cut each chicken breast into nine finger-length strips. Place them in a bowl with the oil and herbs, season well with black pepper and leave to marinate for a minimum of 2 hours.

De-rind the bacon and stretch it flat, using the back of a knife. Spread each rasher with a little mustard, cut into four lengths and roll up, mustard side innermost. Thread a strip of chicken on to each skewer, followed by a roll of bacon, and chill until you're ready to cook them.

To make the dipping sauce, combine all the ingredients, season to taste with salt and pepper and pour into a small bowl.

Heat the grill until very hot. Arrange the kebabs on a baking sheet and wrap the visible parts of the skewers in aluminium foil. Grill the chicken and bacon for 2–3min each side, or until the bacon is brown and the chicken is cooked thoroughly – check that the juices run clear, not pink, when you stab the thickest part of each strip. Arrange kebabs on a large serving dish with the dipping sauce, garnish with the herbs and serve.

Wild Boar Sausage
and Chestnut Tortilla Wraps

MAKES 30

10 wild boar or Cumberland
sausages

2 tbsp tomato purée

1 tbsp dark brown sugar

1 tbsp sesame seeds

10 small flour tortillas

5 tbsp cranberry and port relish
(see page 46)

170g (6oz/³/4 cup) cooked
chestnuts, chopped

1 tsp finely chopped sage

Heat the oven to 190°C (375°F/gas mark 5).

Arrange the sausages in a large roasting tin. Mix the
tomato purée and brown sugar together, then brush
half of this over the sausages. Roast the sausages for
12–15min.

Turn the sausages and brush the second side with the
remaining tomato mixture. Sprinkle the sesame seeds
over the top and season with black pepper. Continue to
roast sausages for a further 12–15min, or until well
cooked and sticky.

Warm the tortillas in the oven for 2min. Lay each
warm tortilla on the work surface and spread each with
a light covering of the cranberry relish. Sprinkle the
chestnuts and sage over the top. Sit one sausage at one
end of the wrap and roll tightly. Trim the ends of each
wrap and then cut into three, on the diagonal. Secure
the wrap with a cocktail stick if necessary. Serve hot or
cold.

Baked Winter Vegetable Wedges with Garlic Mayonnaise

These wedges are fabulous with any creamy dip – classic tartare sauce, or even a good pesto, works very well.

MAKES 30

2 sweet potatoes, peeled and cut into wedges, lengthways

2 parsnips, peeled and cut into wedges, lengthways

1 celeriac, peeled and cut into wedges, from the middle

2 large baking potatoes, scrubbed and cut into wedges, lengthways

1 tbsp chopped rosemary

1 tbsp extra virgin olive oil

2 tbsp freshly grated Parmesan cheese (optional)

$1/2$ tsp cayenne pepper

4 cloves garlic, skins on

150ml ($1/4$ pint/$1/2$ cup) mayonnaise

150ml ($1/4$ pint/$1/2$ cup) Greek yoghurt

2 tbsp chopped chives, to serve

Heat the oven to 200°C (400°F/gas mark 6).

Put the prepared vegetables, rosemary, olive oil, Parmesan cheese, cayenne pepper and garlic into a large plastic bag and season very generously with salt and pepper. Toss together until the vegetables have a light coating of oil and seasoning.

Arrange the vegetables, in a single layer, in a large roasting tin. Bake for 15min, then turn the vegetables over in the tin and remove the garlic. Continue to bake for a further 20–25min, or until vegetables are lightly browned and tender.

In the meantime, crush the roasted garlic and put the flesh into a bowl with the mayonnaise and yoghurt. Add the chives, and season to taste with salt and pepper.

When the vegetables are cooked, place them in a large serving dish and hand the mayonnaise separately.

Potted Red Leicester Cheese with Toasted Hazelnuts

MAKES 30

340g (12oz/3 cups) Red Leicester cheese, grated

55g (2oz/1/4 cup) unsalted butter

110g (4oz/1 cup) cream cheese

2 tbsp fino sherry

1 tbsp capers, rinsed

1/4 tsp ground mace

Celery salt (optional)

1/4 tsp dried English mustard

1/2 tsp cayenne pepper

5 large slices pumpernickel and 55g (2oz/1/2 cup) toasted hazelnuts, roughly chopped, to serve

Place the Red Leicester cheese, butter, cream cheese, sherry and capers in a food processor and whizz together to form a smooth purée. Add the mace, celery salt, mustard and cayenne pepper. Season to taste with salt and pepper and whizz again briefly.

Fill a piping bag, fitted with a 1cm (1/2in) plain nozzle, with the mixture. Pipe rounds on to the slices of pumpernickel bread and sprinkle the hazelnuts on top. Cover and eat within 2 hours.

Lime Chilli Prawns

FOR 30

1kg (2.2lb/4 1/2 cups) cooked and peeled tiger prawns

Grated zest of 3 limes

150ml (1/4 pint/1/2 cup) sweet chilli sauce

2 tbsp lime juice

2 tbsp roughly chopped coriander

Lime wedges, sprigs of coriander and cocktail sticks, to serve

Pat the tiger prawns dry, if necessary, with some absorbent kitchen paper. Place them in a bowl and add the lime zest and plenty of ground black pepper. Leave to marinate for at least 2 hours, in the refrigerator.

Mix the chilli sauce, lime juice and coriander together, and season with salt.

Just before serving, toss the prawns in the chilli dressing and place them on a large serving dish. Decorate with lime wedges and sprigs of coriander, and serve, handing cocktail sticks separately.

Mini Apple and Mincemeat Strudels

MAKES 30

4 red-skinned apples, cored and diced

30g (1oz/⅛ cup) butter

1 tbsp light brown sugar

½ tsp ground cinnamon
110g (4oz/½ cup) Fruit Mincemeat (see page 43)

10 sheets filo pastry

5 tbsp sunflower oil

Cinnamon sticks, to garnish

Place the apples, butter, sugar and cinnamon in a pan and cook over a high heat for 3–4min, or until brown and caramelized. Transfer to a bowl to cool, then mix with the mincemeat and set aside.

Brush one sheet of filo pastry with a little oil and cut it into 7.5cm (3in) strips. Put a spoonful of the apple mixture at one end of each strip and fold the end over the apple to form a triangle. Continue to fold pastry across and over until you reach the end of the strip, so that the apple is completely encased in a triangle. Brush the top of each with a little more oil and arrange on a baking sheet.

Heat the oven to 190°C (375°F/gas mark 5).

Cook strudels on the top shelf of the oven for 10–12min, or until crisp. Transfer to a wire rack to cool for at least 10min before serving.

Dust strudels very heavily with icing sugar, and arrange them on a colourful dish. Decorate with some tied bunches of cinnamon sticks, and serve.

Macadamia Meringue Kisses

MAKES 50

2 egg whites

110g (4oz/$\frac{1}{2}$ cup) caster sugar

85g (3oz/$\frac{3}{4}$ cup) macadamia nuts, freshly ground

For the topping:

110g (4oz/$\frac{1}{2}$ cup) plain dark chocolate

55g (2oz/$\frac{1}{4}$ cup) white chocolate

1 tsp butter

Heat the oven to 140°C (275°F/gas mark 1).

Whisk the egg whites until very stiff. Whisk in the sugar, a teaspoonful at a time, until the meringue is stiff, but glossy – don't add the sugar too quickly or the meringue will become very soft.

Sprinkle the ground nuts on to the meringue and briefly fold them in. Spoon the mixture into a piping bag fitted with a 1cm ($\frac{1}{2}$in) plain nozzle and pipe meringues about 2cm ($\frac{3}{4}$in) wide on to a sheet of non-stick baking parchment.

Bake the meringues on the bottom shelf of the oven for 45min or until they come loose from the paper. Transfer to a wire rack to cool.

To decorate the meringues, melt the plain chocolate in a small bowl over a saucepan of simmering water. Dip the tips of the meringues into the melted chocolate and leave to set.

Melt the white chocolate and butter in the same way and, once melted and cooled, spoon into a piping bag. Drizzle the chocolate across the tops of the meringues in a zigzag pattern and leave to cool before serving.

The meringues can be made at least three days in advance, but they shouldn't be dipped in chocolate until the day that they're required.

Mulled Wine

SERVES 6

2 bottles claret

3 satsumas, thickly sliced

2 lemons, thickly sliced

4 tbsp caster sugar

2 cinnamon sticks

1–2 tsp whole cloves

8 allspice berries, bruised

1 tsp ground ginger

Place all the ingredients in a saucepan and heat over a very low flame until the sugar has dissolved. Bring to the boil and simmer for 5–6min. Remove from the heat and leave to infuse for 5–10min.

Pour the mulled wine into a warm jug and add more sugar, if necessary, to taste. Serve hot.

Fruit Mincemeat

Mincemeat was made in England as far back as the sixteenth century, when spiced savoury minced meat (tongue or beef) was enlivened with spices and fruit. Over the years, most of the 'meat' element has been lost so that, today, many traditional mincemeat recipes are made only from fruit, spices and beef suet. This recipe does not contain beef suet, but has the addition of fresh fruit, meaning that it should be made and used within two to three weeks.

900g (2lb/4^{1}/$_{2}$ cups) mixed dried fruit, such as sultanas, raisins, currants and candied peel

55g (2oz/^{1}/$_{2}$ cup) glacé cherries, chopped

55g (2oz/^{1}/$_{2}$ cup) blanched almonds, chopped

^{1}/$_{2}$ tsp each ground cinnamon, grated nutmeg, ground cloves and mixed spice

Grated zest and juice of 1 lemon and 1 orange

110g (4oz/^{2}/$_{3}$ cup) soft brown sugar

110g (4oz/^{1}/$_{2}$ cup) butter

110g (4oz/^{3}/$_{4}$ cup) tinned pineapple, chopped

1 banana, chopped

1 dessert apple, grated

55g (2oz/^{1}/$_{2}$ cup) each black and white grapes, halved

3 tbsp brandy

Put the dried fruit, cherries, almonds, spices, zest and juice into a bowl. Leave to soak for 2–3 hours, then stir in the sugar.

Melt the butter in a large saucepan, add the tinned and fresh fruit and toss over a high heat for 2–3min. Cool completely, then add it to the dried fruit, along with the brandy.

Cover and store in the refrigerator for no more than a week or freeze for up to 3 months.

Satsuma and Cinnamon Marmalade

If you're unable to find kumquats, you can use a couple of oranges instead.

Makes 5 x 450g (1lb) jars
1kg (2.2lb) satsumas or clementines
3 lemons
225g (8oz) kumquats or 2 oranges
4 sticks cinnamon
2 star anise
3ltr (5^1/$_4$ pints/12^1/$_2$ cups) water
1.35kg (3lbs/6 cups) preserving sugar
Jam jars and covers

Squeeze the juice from the satsumas and lemons and strain it into a large bowl, scooping out as much membrane and pith as possible. Put membrane, pith and pips on to a piece of muslin, tie it securely into a bag and add the bag and skins to the bowl of juice.

Cut the kumquats in half and remove as many small pips as possible. Add the fruit to the bowl of juice and skins, along with the cinnamon sticks, star anise and water. Leave to soak for 2 hours.

Transfer the soaking skins and pulp mixture to a large saucepan or preserving pan, bring the liquid to the boil and simmer for 1^1/$_2$ hours, or until the fruit skins are soft. Lift the muslin bag out of the liquid, squeeze it to remove excess juice and then discard it. Shred the satsuma and lemon skins, slice the halved kumquats and put them all back into the saucepan with the sugar.

Heat the mixture gently until the sugar has dissolved, then boil it rapidly for 20–30min, or until the marmalade reaches setting point.

To test whether setting point is reached, put a small spoonful of marmalade on to a saucer and chill for 5min – it's done if a thick skin forms and wrinkles when you push a spoon through it.

Once the setting point is reached, remove the saucepan from the heat and strain off any surface residue with a slotted spoon. Leave the marmalade to cool for 30min.

To sterilize the jam jars, heat the oven to 100°C (200°F/gas mark ^{1}/$_2$). Wash jars in hot, soapy water, then place them, upside down on a baking sheet, in the oven to dry.

Transfer the cooled marmalade to a jug and divide between the jam jars. Cover each with a wax disc and cellophane secured with an elastic band. Label the jars when cold. Keep in a cool dark place for a couple of weeks before eating.

Marzipan Mince Pies

If you prefer, substitute Fruit Mincemeat (see page 43) for the mincemeat recipe here.

MAKES 24

For the pastry:

225g (8oz/1¼ cups) plain flour

110g (4oz/½ cup) butter

55g (2oz/½ cup) ground almonds

2 tbsp caster sugar

1 egg yolk

3–4 tbsp cold water

For the mincemeat:

85g (3oz/⅔ cup) dried cranberries

2 tbsp rum

55g (2oz/¼ cup) glacé cherries, chopped

55g (2oz/¼ cup) candied peel, chopped

110g (4oz/½ cup) dried figs, chopped

110g (4oz/½ cup) dried apricots, finely sliced

55g (2oz/½ cup) hazelnuts, toasted and chopped

1 x 200g (7oz/1¼ cups) tinned crushed pineapple

1 dessert apple, peeled and chopped

225g (8oz/1 cup) marzipan

Icing sugar, to serve

To make the pastry: Sift the flour into a large bowl. Rub the butter into the flour until the mixture resembles fine breadcrumbs, then add the ground almonds and sugar, and stir. Mix the egg yolk and water together, add to the flour mixture and stir to form a soft, but not sticky, dough. Knead the dough lightly, then wrap and chill it for 15min before use.

Roll out the pastry to 3mm (⅛in), then cut out 24 rounds, using a fluted cutter. Line one or more tartlet tins with the rounds, then chill the pastry for a further 30min.

To make the mincemeat: Soak the cranberries in the rum for 15min. Mix the remaining ingredients together and leave to macerate for 30min.

Heat the oven to 190ºC (375ºF/gas mark 5). Line the pie rounds with non-stick baking parchment and add dried beans to weight the pastry. Blind bake the pastry cases for 12–15min. Meanwhile, roll out the marzipan to 0.5cm (¼in) and cut out lids for the pies using a star or leaf cutter.

Remove tarts from the oven and place a tablespoon of mincemeat into each, then place a marzipan lid on top. *At this stage, pies can be frozen for up to 3 months.* Dust the tops with icing sugar and set aside until required.

To serve, re-dust with icing sugar, if necessary, and reheat the pies at 150ºC (300ºF/gas mark 2) for 10–12min. Either spoon a little Rum, Orange and Coconut Butter on top of each pie, or hand it separately.

Rum, Orange and Coconut Butter

250g (9oz/1^{1}/8 cup) unsalted butter

110g (4oz/1 cup) icing sugar

2–3 tbsp Malibu or coconut rum

Grated zest of 1 orange

2 tbsp desiccated coconut, toasted

Whizz all the ingredients in a food processor, and serve. The butter will keep for a few days in the refrigerator, or can be stored in the freezer for up to 3 months.

Cranberry and Port Relish

Cranberry or redcurrant jellies are old favourites, but this relish makes a refreshing change.

450g (1lb/2 cups) fresh
cranberries

Juice and grated zest of 1 large
orange

85–110g (3–4oz/³/4–1 cup)
granulated sugar, to taste

250ml (8fl oz/1 cup) water

5 tbsp port

Place the cranberries, orange, most of the sugar and the water in a large pan, cover and cook over a very low heat until the cranberries are just soft. Remove the lid and boil rapidly, stirring continuously, for 7–10min, or until thick and well reduced. Add the port and more sugar to taste, and leave to cool.

The relish will keep for a few days in the refrigerator, or can be frozen for up to 3 months.

Christmas Stollen

Stollen is a Christmas speciality from Germany and can be found all around Europe. As with panettone, you can buy some fantastic stollen in many supermarkets these days, but it's fun to make if you have the time and inclination. It's traditionally shaped into a long folded oval with a strip of marzipan through the middle, which is said to represent the infant Jesus wrapped in swaddling clothes. This, however, is a non-traditional, easy version.

450g (1lb/2 cups) plain flour

3 level tsp baking powder

170g (6oz/³/₄ cup) caster sugar

2 tsp vanilla essence

1 tsp almond essence

2 tbsp rum

Grated zest and juice of 1 lemon

1 tsp mixed spice

2 eggs

170g (6oz/³/₄ cup) unsalted butter, softened

225g (8oz/1 cup) smetana or low fat soured cream

110g (4oz/²/₃ cup) candied peel, roughly chopped

55g (2oz/¹/₃ cup) raisins

55g (2oz/¹/₃ cup) sultanas

110g (4oz/1 cup) toasted hazelnuts

225g (8oz/1 cup) marzipan

Icing sugar, to finish

Heat the oven to 180°C (350°F/gas mark 4).

Sift the flour and baking powder into a large bowl and add the caster sugar. Put the essences, rum, lemon zest and juice, mixed spice and eggs into a bowl and beat together. Add the softened butter and smetana, and stir.

Add the egg mixture to the flour, together with the candied peel, raisins, sultanas and hazelnuts and mix to a dough. Roll or press the dough into an oval shape and place on a lightly greased baking tray. Bake for 20min, then reduce the oven temperature to 170°C (325°F/gas mark 3) and bake for a further 20–25min, or until the base sounds hollow when tapped.

Remove the stollen from the tin and leave to cool on a wire rack. Roll the marzipan to fit the top of the stollen. Press onto the surface then dust generously with icing sugar and serve.

Chestnut, Chocolate and Mincemeat Semi-freddo Pudding

A great alternative to Christmas pudding.

SERVES 8

300g (11 oz/1¾ cups) dark chocolate

200ml (7½ fl oz/1 cup) double cream

3 tbsp Grand Marnier or brandy (a miniature)

1 x 400g (14oz/1⅔ cups) tin of sweetened chestnut purée

Juice and grated zest of 1 orange

225g (8oz/1 heaped cup) cooked chestnuts, chopped

225g (8oz/1 heaped cup) Fruit Mincemeat (see page 43)

Chop the dark chocolate and place it in a bowl over simmering water with 3 tbsp of double cream and 1 tbsp Grand Marnier. Stir the ingredients together until just melted (do not overheat). Leave to cool.

Put the chestnut purée into a food processor and whizz with the orange juice and zest until smooth. Pour the mixture into a bowl and stir in the chestnuts, mincemeat and remaining Grand Marnier.

Whip the remaining cream until it just holds its shape and fold it, with the cool chocolate, into the chestnut mixture. Pour the mixture into a 1ltr (1¾ pint) loaf tin, lined with a double strip of lightly oiled greaseproof paper, and wrap the tin well in aluminium foil. Freeze for at least 4 hours. Remove the pudding from the freezer and leave it to soften in the refrigerator about 1 hour before serving.

To serve, run a warm knife down the sides of the pudding and invert it on to a plate. Cut into slices using a warm serrated knife. Decorate the plate with Grand Marnier Clementines.

After dinner petit fours

If you have any room for them, a tray of petit fours is a festive and colourful way to conclude the Christmas meal. Serve them with coffee and Frosted Fruit (see page 65).

Three-chocolate Truffles

150ml (¼ pint/⅝ cup) double cream

55g (2oz/¼ cup) unsalted butter

225g (8oz/1 cup) dark chocolate (minimum 70% cocoa solids), chopped

110g (4oz/½ cup) milk chocolate, chopped

2 tbsp Cointreau or Grand Marnier (optional)

170g (6oz/¾ cup) white chocolate, melted, to decorate

Petit four cases

Heat the double cream and butter to scalding point and pour into a glass bowl.

Add the dark and milk chocolate and stir until melted (it may be necessary to warm the bowl a little to make sure the chocolate melts completely, but don't allow the chocolate to get too hot).

Add the liqueur (if using) to the mixture and leave to cool, then chill for 1 hour.

Scoop the cold mixture into balls using a melon (Parisienne) baller. Alternatively, fill a piping bag, fitted with a 2.5cm (1in) plain nozzle, with the mixture and pipe long strips on to greaseproof paper, cut the strips into 2.5cm (1in) lengths.

Put the truffles into petit four cases and chill until you're ready to decorate them. To decorate, fill a piping bag with cooled, melted chocolate and pipe swirls and stripes across the truffles. Arrange in gift boxes or bags (if using) and keep chilled.

Caramel Spiced Nuts

110g (4oz/1 cup) Brazil nuts

110g (4oz/1 cup) cashew nuts

110g (4oz/1 cup) unblanched almonds

110g (4oz/1 cup) walnuts

1 tbsp sunflower oil

1 tsp garam masala

1 tsp ground ginger

1 tsp ground cinnamon

3 tbsp sesame seeds

1 tbsp poppy seeds

170g (6oz/¾ cup) granulated sugar

150ml (¼ pint/½ cup) boiling water

Heat the oven to 190ºC (375ºF/gas mark 5).

Place the nuts on a baking sheet and toast in the oven for 10–12min, or until lightly browned. Tip them on to a plate to cool.

Heat the oil in a small frying pan and add the spices, sesame seeds and poppy seeds. Toss them over a low to medium heat until the sesame seeds are lightly toasted. Spread seeds on to a large plate and leave to cool.

Put the sugar and water into a heavy-based saucepan. Heat slowly until the sugar has dissolved, then bring the liquid to the boil and cook until a toffee-coloured syrup has formed. Remove from the heat and allow the bubbles to subside, but don't allow to cool.

Add the nuts to the syrup and stir until lightly coated, then remove them and roll in the sesame seeds until covered. Place the nuts individually on a large sheet of non-stick baking parchment and leave them to set for 15min.

Store the caramel nuts in an airtight container for a couple of days. To giftwrap, place a handful in clear cellophane and tie with ribbon. They will keep for a week.

Candied Citrus Peel

Candied peel is a traditional favourite at Christmas – it takes a little time to prepare, but makes a great after-dinner sweet nibble. It can also be chopped and used as part of many festive recipes, including Fruit Mincemeat and Traditional Rich Fruit Cake (see pages 43 and 30), but if you're short of time, you can use ready-made candied peel in these recipes. Although candied peel is traditionally made with citron, a type of lemon, this is hard to come by nowadays, so standard lemons are used here.

MAKES 340–450G (12OZ–1LB)

The peel of 2 oranges, 2 lemons, 2 limes and 3 tangerines, well washed to remove any wax

400g (14oz/2³/4 cups) granulated sugar

Caster sugar, to dust

110g (4oz/¹/2 cup) dark chocolate, melted

Trim the excess pith from the citrus skins and cut the peel into strips 1cm (¹/2in) wide and 5cm (2in) long. Put the pith into a large bowl and cover with water. Leave to soak overnight.

The next day, place the peel and soaking water from the pith into a large saucepan. Bring to the boil and simmer for 45min, or until the peel is soft. Lift the peel out with a slotted spoon and place in a bowl. Add the sugar to the remaining cooking liquid and stir. Bring it to the boil over a low heat until dissolved, replace the peel and simmer for 15min.

Transfer the peel and syrup to a bowl and leave to soak overnight. Repeat the boiling, simmering and cooling process the following day.

Remove the peel from the syrup and roll the strips in the caster sugar. Leave to dry on a piece of non-stick baking parchment.

To use as petits fours, dip the ends of some of the strips in melted chocolate and leave to set. Serve these on their own or as an accompaniment to creamy or citrus desserts.

Mini Ginger Melting Moments

MAKES 25

110g (4oz/¹/₂ cup) block margarine

45g (1¹/₂ oz/¹/₃ cup) icing sugar, sifted

30g (1oz/¹/₄ cup) cornflour

155g (5¹/₂ oz/1 cup plus 1 tbsp) plain flour

1 tsp ground ginger

Pinch of salt

110g (4oz/¹/₂ cup) unsalted butter

Juice and grated zest of ¹/₂ lemon

2 tbsp icing sugar, plus extra for dusting

Heat the oven to 150ºC (300ºF/gas mark 2).

Cream the margarine and icing sugar together until soft. Sift the cornflour, flour, ginger and salt together and work into the mixture to form a soft dough.

Shape the dough into walnut-sized balls. Arrange these on a baking sheet, pressing the tops lightly with a fork to flatten the top and base. Chill for 10min and then bake for 15–18min, or until firm, but not brown. Transfer to a wire rack to cool.

Cream together the butter, lemon juice, zest and icing sugar. Use this mixture to sandwich two Melting Moments together. Arrange on a plate, dust with icing sugar and serve. To giftwrap, place a handful of Melting Moments on a piece of clear cellophane, gather into a parcel and tie with ribbon.

CHRISTMAS EVE

Christmas Eve, 24 December, is the day for celebrating Jesus's birth and exchanging gifts in many countries across Europe. Midnight and a holy communion service heralds the birth of Christ as it has done for centuries – this is one of the best-attended church services of the year.

Fish is particularly popular and traditional at this time, especially in Scandinavia where smorgasbords with an assortment of preserved herring, cod, mackerel and the traditional lutefisk are served.

Coarse fish such as carp, perch, pike and zander, and river trout are an important part of the everyday diet of landlocked countries across Europe, including Poland and Austria. Many European countries serve a traditional baked carp as their celebration meal on Christmas Eve.

The birth of Christ at midnight heralds the start of the Christmas season of twelve days.

CHRISTMAS EVE SUPPER

SERVES 6

Gravadlax with Dill and Lime

Seafood and Saffron Cannelloni

Warm Winter Fruit Compôte

To complete the menu, serve a crisp winter leaf salad with the cannelloni, Treacle Snaps (see page 150) with the compôte, and a zingy New Zealand Sauvignon Blanc.

Gravadlax with Dill and Lime

SERVES 6

For the dressing:

2 tbsp chopped dill

2 tbsp Dijon mustard

1 tbsp dark brown sugar

1 tbsp white wine vinegar

150ml ($^{1}/_{4}$ pint/$^{1}/_{2}$ cup) Greek yoghurt

Grated zest of 1 lime

12 slices of gravadlax or smoked salmon

1 x 70g (2$^{1}/_{2}$ oz/$^{1}/_{4}$ cup) pot salmon roe (keta)

Melba toast or blinis

2 limes, each cut into 6 wedges

Sprigs of dill, to garnish

To make the dressing, combine all the ingredients and season to taste with salt and pepper – add more sugar and a splash of lime juice if desired. Transfer to a small serving bowl.

Fold the gravadlax or smoked salmon slices in half and arrange on a large platter.

Spoon the salmon roe over the gravadlax and arrange the lime wedges and Melba toast or blinis around the edge. Decorate with sprigs of dill, and serve. Hand the dressing separately.

Seafood and Saffron Cannelloni

SERVES 6

1 leek, finely sliced

1 head of Florence fennel, very finely sliced

3 tbsp olive oil

2 cloves garlic, crushed

1 tbsp tomato purée

1 rounded tbsp flour

1/2 tsp Madras curry powder

A large pinch of saffron

Grated zest of 1 orange

225ml (1/3 pint/2/3 cup) fish stock

300ml (1/2 pint/1 cup) crème fraîche

2 tbsp finely chopped parsley

225g (8oz) cod fillet, skinned

225g (8oz) monkfish tail, skinned

225g (8oz) lemon sole fillet, skinned

3 scallops

3 whole squid, cleaned

170g (6oz) cooked tiger prawns

A little flour seasoned with salt, pepper and cayenne

12 sheets of lasagne verde, cooked al dente

1 egg, beaten

4 tbsp freshly grated Parmesan cheese

2 tbsp dried white breadcrumbs

Cook the leek and fennel in the olive oil for 10–12min, or until soft (don't allow it to burn). Add the garlic, tomato purée, flour, curry powder and saffron, and cook for a further 1min. Stir the orange zest and stock into the vegetables, bring to the boil and simmer for 10min. Season to taste with salt and pepper. Add 2 tbsp of the crème fraîche and the chopped parsley. Set aside to cool completely.

Cut the cod, monkfish and lemon sole fillets into 4cm (1½in) chunks. Trim the scallops, removing the muscle and membrane from around the edge. Detach the roe from the main flesh and split it in half, if necessary. Cut the squid into thin strips and cut the prawns in half. Toss the fish (not the shellfish) in the seasoned flour and stir it into the cold sauce along with the shellfish.

Heat the oven to 180ºC (350ºF/gas mark 4).

Lay the lasagne sheets on a clean work surface. Divide the fish mixture between each sheet and roll up to form cannelloni. Arrange cannelloni, seam side down, in a large, buttered gratin dish.

Mix the remaining crème fraîche with the egg, season to taste with salt, pepper and nutmeg, and spoon over the cannelloni. Sprinkle the Parmesan cheese and breadcrumbs over the top and bake for 30–35min, or until the fish is cooked and the top is golden brown. Serve very hot.

Warm Winter Fruit Compôte

This compôte looks sensational piled high in tall, individual glasses. Serve it with warm Marzipan Mince Pies (see page 44) or Petits Fours.

Serves 6

12 physalis, peeled and washed

4 persimmons (Sharon fruit), peeled

6 kumquats, thinly sliced

225g (8oz/1 cup) large dates, halved and stoned

110g (4oz/1/2 cup) black grapes, pips removed

225g (8oz/1 cup) seedless green grapes

2 ripe pomegranates

300ml (1/2 pint/1 1/4 cups) apple juice

150ml (1/4 pint/5/8 cup) dry cider (optional)

2 sticks cinnamon

6 star anise

6 whole cardamom pods

6 black peppercorns

1 tsp coriander seeds

300ml (1/2 pint/1 1/4 cup) fromage frais, to serve

Cut the physalis in half and place in a large glass bowl. Cut the persimmons into wedges and add to the physalis, with the kumquats, dates and grapes. Cut the pomegranates in half and remove the seeds, taking care to remove all the pith, as this is very bitter.

Place the apple juice and cider in a saucepan with the cinnamon and star anise. Tie up the cardamom, peppercorns and coriander seeds in a small piece of muslin and add the bag to the pan. On a low heat, bring the juice very slowly to the boil and then immediately remove it from the heat. Leave to infuse for 10min.

Remove the muslin bag and pour the juice over the fruit and leave it to stand for 5min. Serve in tall glasses, with a bowl of fromage frais on the side.

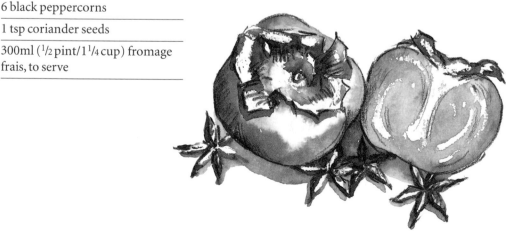

CHRISTMAS DAY

Probably the best-known date in the Church calendar, Christmas Day, 25 December, is a joyful time of sharing and giving. In pre-Christian days, the pagan festival of the winter solstice fell during the bitterly cold weather of late December and January when the weather made agricultural work very hard. The Christian Church chose this time to celebrate the birth of Christ – the word 'Christmas' means the Mass of Christ. Not only did Christmas encompass the pagan festivities, but the time just after the winter solstice, when the days are at their shortest, was also a good time to 'bring light to the world' with the celebration of the birth of Jesus. It became a twelve-day holiday, which was just what those working on the land needed.

In Britain today, it's traditional to celebrate Christmas Day with a roast turkey and 'all the trimmings', while a baked glazed ham is the usual fare in many European countries – traditions that were established in the nineteenth century. Before turkey was introduced in Britain, roast capon, goose or beef was the order of the day. Today's equivalent of capon – a castrated cockerel, no longer available – is a very large chicken. Chicken is commonplace nowadays and is eaten at any time of the week, so it's easy to forget that, until recently, it was one of the most expensive meats around and was kept as a Sunday treat.

If you prefer to cook a goose, a pheasant or beef for Christmas lunch, the recipes can be found under other feast celebrations in this book.

CHRISTMAS DAY BREAKFAST

Smoked Salmon and Quail's Egg Kedgeree
Festive Muffins

I have spent several Christmases in the southern hemisphere, where we would start the day with smoked salmon and scrambled egg or kedgeree, warm muffins or croissants and a glass of bubbly. For an extra fizz, serve some champagne cocktails, made with a few sugar cubes, a couple of drops of angostura bitters and a measure of brandy, topped up with non-vintage champagne – fantastic!

Stilton, Persimmon and Toasted Walnut Salad
Ginger and Maple Glazed Ham
Char-grilled Turkey with Mushroom and Marsala Sauce
or Chestnut and Herb Roast Turkey (see page 232)
Braised Red Cabbage with Honey and Apricots
Panettone, Chocolate and Marmalade Puddings
Grand Marnier Clementines
or Old-fashioned Boiled Plum Pudding (see page 29)
or Chestnut, Chocolate and Mincemeat Semi-freddo Pudding (see page 48)
Frosted Fruit
or After-Dinner Petits Fours

Serve the ham or turkey with roast potatoes or Roast Garlic and Olive Oil Mash (see page 234), Brussels sprouts and Cranberry and Port Relish (see page 46).

A really good Barolo from northern Italy is a lovely accompaniment, and if you've opted for the traditional Christmas pudding, serve it with a glass of old tawny port.

Smoked Salmon and Quail's Egg Kedgeree

SERVES 6

1 dozen quail's eggs

225g (8oz/1 heaped cup) basmati rice, cooked and drained

55g (2oz/¼ cup) butter

½ tsp ground cinnamon

½ tsp garam masala

½ tsp ground ginger

¼ tsp ground turmeric

8 spring onions, finely sliced

110g (4oz/1 cup) smoked salmon trimmings

A squeeze of lemon juice

1 tbsp chopped parsley

Cook the eggs in boiling water for 5min until hard-boiled. Drain and crack the shells of each egg and submerge them in cold water. Peel and cut each egg in half, and set aside.

Cook the basmati rice in boiling water for 10–12min until tender. Drain and pat dry with absorbent paper.

Melt the butter in a large frying pan, add the spices and fry for 30 seconds. Add the spring onions and toss them over a medium heat for 1 min. Turn the heat down, add the rice and cook until it's very hot.

Add the smoked salmon, quail's eggs and lemon juice to the rice and stir. Season to taste with salt and pepper, then add the chopped parsley. Heat for a further min and spoon on to a serving dish.

Festive Muffins

Makes 8–10

225g (8oz/1³/₈ cups) plain flour

2 tsp baking powder

1 tsp ground cinnamon

1 tsp mixed spice

1 tsp ground ginger

2 large eggs, beaten

85g (3oz/³/₈ cup) butter, melted and cooled

200ml (7fl oz/⁷/₈ cup) buttermilk

100g (3¹/₂oz/¹/₂ cup) light brown sugar

100g (3¹/₂oz/¹/₂ cup) dried cranberries

100g (3¹/₂oz/¹/₂ cup) dried blueberries

1 dessert apple, coarsely grated

3–4 tbsp mincemeat

A splash of brandy

Heat the oven to 190ºC (375ºF/gas mark 5).

Sift the flour, baking powder, cinnamon, mixed spice and ginger into a large bowl. Make a well in the centre and add the eggs, butter, buttermilk and sugar. Stir these into the flour.

Add the fruit, mincemeat and brandy, then mix together. Divide the mixture between 8 or 10 paper muffin cases, placed in a muffin tin. Bake for 25–30min, or until well-risen and golden brown. Serve warm or cold.

Stilton, Persimmon and Toasted Walnut Salad

This is a colourful and festive salad created by a friend, Joan Ashworth.

SERVES 8–10

170g (6oz/1 1/2 cup) Stilton cheese, crumbled

5 ripe persimmons (Sharon fruit), peeled and diced

A large selection of salad leaves, such as Cos lettuce, curly endive and radicchio, washed

55g (2oz/1/4 cup) butter

4 tbsp demerara sugar

110g (4oz/1 cup) walnuts, roughly chopped

For the dressing:

8 tbsp sunflower oil

2–3 tbsp white wine vinegar

1 tsp English mustard

Place the Stilton cheese, persimmons and lettuce leaves in a large bowl and set aside.

Place the butter and sugar in a large frying pan, add the walnuts and cook them over a brisk heat for 3–4min, or until caramelized. Transfer the nuts to a plate and leave to cool.

Mix the dressing ingredients together, season to taste with salt and pepper and whisk well.

Add the nuts to the salad, along with the dressing, and toss together well. Transfer to a clean salad bowl and serve immediately.

Ginger and Maple Glazed Ham

SERVES 8-10

2kg (4.4lb) ham joint

1 onion, halved

6 whole cloves

1 carrot, peeled and sliced

2 sticks celery

600ml (1 pint/2^1/2 cups) dry cider

6 pieces stem ginger, chopped

5 tbsp maple syrup

1 tsp dried English mustard

1–2 tsp Sichuan peppercorns (or whole cloves)

Soak the ham in cold water for 24 hours, then discard the liquid. Place the meat in a large saucepan and add the onion, cloves, carrot and celery. Bring to the boil, reduce the heat and simmer for 2–2^1/4 hours, or until the ham is cooked and the skin is loose. Lift the meat out and peel away the skin, leaving a thin layer of fat. If the rind doesn't peel away easily, the ham needs to cook a little longer. Strain the cooking liquid and reserve it for soup-making (see Ham and Puy Lentil Soup on page 73).

Heat the oven to 180°C (350°F/gas mark 4).

Place the ham in a roasting tin and pour the cider around the base. Mix the chopped ginger, syrup and mustard together and spread the paste across the top and sides of the ham. Sprinkle the peppercorns over the top or stud the ham with the cloves. Bake for 35–40min, or until the glaze has become sticky and brown, brushing the cooking juices over the surface during cooling to ensure a sticky glaze forms. Serve the ham hot or cold.

Char-grilled Turkey with Mushroom and Marsala Sauce

If you're cooking for a small party over Christmas, this turkey recipe is a little different and makes a quick alternative to roasting a whole bird.

SERVES 4

4 x 200g (7oz) turkey escalopes (cut from the breast)

1 tbsp sunflower oil

55g (2oz/^{1}/$_2$ cup) unsalted butter

340g (12oz/3 cups) chestnut mushrooms, wiped and quartered

2 tbsp Marsala or Madeira

2 tbsp port

5 tbsp chicken or turkey stock

4 tbsp whipping cream

1 tbsp cranberry relish or jelly

1 tsp chopped thyme

Sprigs of thyme, to serve

Trim the membrane off the turkey escalopes, brush with sunflower oil and season with salt and pepper. Set aside.

Melt the butter in a large frying pan until it's very hot and foaming. Add the mushrooms and stir-fry over a high heat for 4–5min, or until just cooked.

Add the Marsala and port and cook for 2min, then add the stock, cream and cranberry relish. Bring to the boil and simmer for 2–3min, or until the sauce is well reduced. Season with salt and pepper, and add the thyme.

Heat a griddle pan until very hot and char-grill the turkey escalopes for 3–4min on each side, or until cooked through. Avoid the temptation to turn the poultry over more than once, as this will erase the clear char-grill pattern.

Arrange a cooked escalope on each plate, spoon the sauce over the top and serve immediately, garnished with thyme.

Braised Red Cabbage with Honey and Apricots

SERVES 8

2 tbsp extra virgin olive oil

1 large red cabbage, finely shredded

2 red onions, finely sliced

110g (4oz/1 cup) dried apricots, finely sliced

4 tbsp balsamic vinegar

225ml (8fl oz/1 cup) water

1 bay leaf

1 tbsp chopped thyme

Honey to taste

Heat the oven to 150°C (300°F/gas mark 2).

Heat the oil in a large casserole pot and gently fry the cabbage and onion for 4–5min. Add the apricots, balsamic vinegar and water and bring to the boil, then add the bay leaf and thyme. Season with salt and pepper. Cover the pot, transfer to the oven and cook for 1¹/₂–2 hours, stirring occasionally and adding a little more water if necessary.

Once cooked, remove from the oven and reduce down most of the liquid in the casserole pot by boiling it rapidly. Add the honey to taste, adjust the seasoning and serve.

Panettone, Chocolate and Marmalade Puddings

Panettone is an Italian speciality bread available in many grocers and delicatessens.

MAKES 8

6 tbsp orange marmalade

4 tbsp Amaretto

3 tbsp mascarpone cheese

5 slices of panettone

110g (4oz/1 cup) dark chocolate, chopped

425ml (3/4 pint/2 cups) milk

3 whole eggs

2 egg yolks

A pinch of ground cinnamon

1 tsp cocoa powder and a little demerara sugar, to serve

Heat the oven to 170ºC (325ºF/gas mark 3).

Mix the marmalade and Amaretto together and divide between eight ramekins.

Spread the mascarpone cheese on each slice of panettone and cut into 2.5cm (1in) pieces. Divide these between the ramekins and sprinkle the chocolate on top of each.

Place the milk, eggs, yolks and cinnamon in a bowl and mix well. Strain the liquid into a jug, pour into the ramekins and leave to soak for 10min.

Place the ramekins in a large roasting tin and pour enough boiling water into the tin to come two-thirds of the way up the sides of the ramekins. Bake on the lowest shelf of the oven for 30–35min, or until the custard is set.

Remove puddings from the oven and sprinkle with the cocoa powder and a heavy dusting of demerara sugar. Serve the puddings hot, warm or cold.

Grand Marnier Clementines

These are a lovely accompaniment to rich puddings or ice cream, and should be made 2 hours before serving.

SERVES 8

12 clementines, tangerines or satsumas

3 tbsp Grand Marnier

1 tsp ground cinnamon

Peel 8 clementines and slice in half through the equator. Arrange the halves on a large flat plate.

Squeeze the juice from the remaining clementines and pour it over the cut fruit. Drizzle the Grand Marnier over and sprinkle the cinnamon on top. Leave to soak for 2 hours at room temperature before serving.

Frosted Fruit

A delicate, sparkling after-dinner treat, these should be prepared at least 2 hours in advance.

110g (4oz/1 cup) physalis

110g (4oz/1 cup) black grapes

110g (4oz/1 cup) green grapes

3 egg whites

Plenty of caster sugar or glucose powder

Peel the papery lantern jacket away from the physalis to reveal the bright orange flesh. Wash and dry all the fruit and remove stalks and pips from the grapes.

Brush the fruit with egg white and dust very generously with sugar. Place on a sheet of non-stick baking parchment and leave to set and 'frost' – this may take up to 2 hours, but can also be done a day in advance.

Arrange in a pile and use to decorate the table or serve with Petits Fours.

THE FEAST OF ST STEPHEN
BOXING DAY

The feast of St Stephen falls on 26 December, but the term Boxing Day sprang from the tradition in Britain of putting aside the day after Christmas to box up leftover food for the poor, and to distribute the collections in church alms boxes to the needy.

Boxing Day is a bank holiday in some countries and is often spent in sporting activity, weather permitting, in order to work off the excesses of the previous day. It's also a time to address the fridge and decide how to use up the leftovers from Christmas Day. It may sound unappealing, but leftovers can be transformed into some great meals, which take little time to prepare. Before Christmas, stock up on extra vegetables and salad leaves to add interest to leftover dishes during the holiday.

Any of the recipes suggested here can be served with a light red wine from the Loire, such as a Chinon.

Turkey, Stilton and Cranberry Crumble

This can be prepared ahead of time. Make sure that the sauce and all the other ingredients are completely cold before you put them with the turkey.

SERVES 6

225g (8oz/1¼ cups) couscous, soaked in boiling water

1 tbsp chopped herbs

3 tbsp extra virgin olive oil

900g (2lb) turkey meat (skin and gristle removed), diced

4 tbsp cranberry relish or jelly

2 tbsp port (optional)

1 leek, finely chopped

30g (1oz/⅛ cup) butter

2 tbsp flour

150ml (¼ pint/⅝ cup) milk

225ml (8fl oz/1 cup) chicken or turkey stock

85g (3oz/⅔ cup) Stilton cheese, crumbled

Preheat the oven to 190ºC (375ºF/gas mark 5).

Drain the couscous and pat dry with absorbent paper. Add the herbs and one tablespoon of olive oil, season to taste with salt and pepper, and set aside.

Combine the turkey pieces with the cranberry relish and port, and set aside.

Heat the remaining olive oil in a large saucepan, add the leek and cook over a low heat for 7–10min, or until soft. Add the butter and stir until melted. Add the flour and cook, stirring, for a further 1min. Gradually add the milk and stock, stirring until it blends with the flour to form a sauce, then bring to the boil and simmer for 2min. Add the cheese and stir until melted. Season the sauce with salt and pepper.

Add the turkey to the sauce, then pour the mixture into a large pie dish. Spoon the couscous over the top and put the dish on to a baking tray. Bake for 30–35min, or until the couscous is lightly browned and the turkey filling is piping hot. Serve immediately with a simple green salad.

Red Thai Vegetable Curry

Even if you don't have lots of leftover cooked vegetables after Christmas day, you can use anything to hand – just adapt the cooking time to suit raw or cooked vegetables.

Serves 6

1 large onion, finely sliced

1 tbsp sunflower oil

1 clove garlic (optional)

2.5cm (1in) piece of galangal (if available) or root ginger, peeled and chopped

1–2 tbsp red Thai curry paste, according to taste

425ml (³/4 pint/2¹/2 cups) tinned tomatoes

300ml (¹/2 pint/1¹/4 cups) coconut milk

A selection of vegetables weighing a total of 1kg (2.2lb), such as potatoes, sweet potatoes, parsnips, pumpkins, Brussels sprouts and carrots, all peeled

Plenty of chopped basil, to garnish

Heat the oil and fry the onion for 20–25min, or until completely soft. Add the garlic, galangal and curry paste and cook for a further 1min. Add the tomatoes and coconut milk, bring to the boil and simmer over a low heat for 10–15min.

Add the vegetables and bring to the boil, then reduce the heat and cook for 25min, or until the vegetables are cooked, or 5min if reheating. Season to taste with salt and pepper. Sprinkle with the basil leaves, and serve with jasmine rice.

Chestnut and Brussels Sprouts Bubble and Squeak

SERVES 6

3 large baking potatoes, scrubbed

110g (4oz/1 cup) cooked chestnuts

450g (1lb/4 cups) cooked Brussels sprouts

1 tsp ground nutmeg

55g (2oz/¼ cup) butter

12 rashers back bacon, rind removed

Heat the oven to 190°C (375°F/gas mark 5).

Stab the potatoes with a knife, then bake for 1 hour, or until tender.

Cut them open, scoop out the flesh and push it through a sieve. Finely chop the skins.

Chop the chestnuts and Brussels sprouts roughly and mix with the potato flesh and skins. Season very well with salt and pepper, then stir in the nutmeg.

Melt the butter in a frying pan until very hot and foaming. Add the potato and the remaining butter and fry over a low heat for 10–12min, breaking the mix into pieces, then flip them over to brown the second side. Continue to cook for a further 4–5min, or until the bubble and squeak is piping hot.

Meanwhile, fry the bacon rashers in a separate frying pan for 2–3min on each side, or until cooked to taste.

Divide the bubble and squeak between six plates and top with the bacon rashers. Serve immediately.

NEW YEAR CELEBRATIONS

The festival of New Year is not a Church feast, but is based on the pagan rituals of the sun – the ringing out of the old and the ringing in of the new in the hope of divine intervention and a good, prosperous year ahead. Many New Year traditions across Europe are rooted in efforts to ensure good fortune in the coming year.

Scots celebrate Hogmanay (New Year) with a ceilidh or party and an evening of feasting – drams of whisky are enjoyed, as is cloutie dumpling (a boiled pudding similar to plum pudding, the 'clout' being the cloth the pudding was boiled in). The ritual of 'first footing', an important part of Hogmanay, takes place after midnight. To bring good fortune to your neighbours it's customary to send a tall, dark male to visit, usually with some salt and a piece of coal or peat.

Lentils are considered by some to be a sign of good wealth and fortune: it's therefore customary to eat a lentil dish at New Year. It is also a family time and we enjoy a family lunch and evening dinner for New Year's Day. You may well want to prepare these ahead of time.

The soup can be made and frozen, as can the Venison Tourtière. The Pomegranate and Lychee Brulées and Clementine Caramel Creams would benefit from being made the day before.

Not a biblical feast – but a day of celebration for the whole family with hopes of a good year ahead.

NEW YEAR'S EVE DINNER

SERVES 6

Smoked Salmon and Dill Tart

Ballotine of Pheasant with Cranberries

Pomegranate and Lychee Brulée

To complete the menu, serve some seasonal vegetables with the pheasant, such as Braised Red Cabbage with Apricots (see page 63), Glazed Jerusalem Artichokes (see page 219) and Yam and Onion Boulangère (see page 233), and serve Mini Ginger Melting Moments (see page 52) with the brulée.

To accompany the dinner and welcome in the New Year, serve a sparkling Saumur.

NEW YEAR'S DAY LUNCH

SERVES 6

Ham and Puy Lentil Soup

Rich Venison Tourtière

Warm Ruby Chard Salad

Clementine Caramel Creams

Serve the soup with Oat and Sunflower Rolls (see page 98) and the venison with Baked Pumpkin (see page 214) and Skewered Jackets (see page 219). Serve Honey Tuiles (see page 118) with the Clementine Creams.

A leading 'red Rhone ranger' wine from California is ideal with this lunch.

Smoked Salmon and Dill Tart

This tart can be served hot or cold. Try wafer-thin slices of smoked ham and chopped chives as an alternative filling.

SERVES 6

225g (8oz/1¾ cup) plain flour

55g (2oz/½ cup) coarse cornmeal or polenta

170g (6oz/¾ cup) unsalted butter

1 tbsp dill seeds, crushed

2 egg yolks

5–6 tbsp cold water

1 large onion, finely chopped

30g (1oz/⅛ cup) butter

300ml (½ pint/1¼ cups) soured cream

150ml (¼ pint/⅔ cup) milk

4 eggs

Grated zest of 1 lemon

Squeeze of lemon juice

225g (8oz) smoked salmon trimmings, chopped

2 tbsp chopped dill

A handful of salad leaves, to garnish

Sift the flour and cornmeal together into a large bowl. Cut the butter into pieces and rub into the flour, until it resembles fine breadcrumbs. Add the dill seed and stir.

In a separate bowl, mix together the egg yolks and water, then stir into the flour mixture. Draw together to form a soft, but not sticky dough – add a little more water if the dough feels very dry. Turn dough on to a floured board and knead it lightly, then wrap and refrigerate for 15min.

Heat the oven to 190°C (375°F/gas mark 5).

Heat the butter in a pan and fry the onion until soft, then tip it into a bowl to cool. Add the soured cream, milk and eggs to the onion, and season with salt and pepper. Add the lemon zest, juice, smoked salmon and dill, and mix in. Chill in the refrigerator until required.

Roll out the pastry dough on a floured surface until it's large enough to line a 30cm (12in) flan ring. Blind bake the pastry (top it with a sheet of greaseproof paper which is weighed down with some baking beans) on the top shelf of the oven for 15min, then remove the paper and bake for a further 5min, or until cooked through.

Reduce the oven temperature to 170°C (325°F/gas mark 3).

Pour the filling into the centre of the baked pastry case. Bake for 40–45min, or until the filling is completely set. Transfer tart to a wire rack to cool.

To serve, cut tart into wedges, garnished with salad leaves.

Ballotine of Pheasant with Cranberries

SERVES 6

2 pheasants, boned

4 chicken thighs, skin removed

2 shallots, peeled

2 cloves garlic, crushed

4 tbsp dried cranberries

2 tbsp pine nuts, toasted

2 tbsp finely chopped parsley

2 tsp finely chopped sage

6 tbsp couscous, soaked in 5 tbsp boiling water

2 squares of muslin, approximately 30x30cm (12x12in)

5 tbsp sunflower oil

4 bay leaves

4 tbsp Marsala

450ml ($^{3}/_{4}$ pint/$2^{1}/_{2}$ cup) chicken stock

1–2 tbsp arrowroot

Remove any thick sinews from the pheasant legs and season the birds with salt and pepper. Cut the chicken meat from the bone.

Put the chicken into a food processor with the shallots, garlic, cranberries, pine nuts and herbs. Whizz in short bursts until the meat is very well minced and the cranberries chopped.

Drain the couscous and pat it dry with absorbent kitchen paper. Add to the chicken mix and whizz in the same way until it's mixed well in. Season with salt and pepper.

Heat the oven to 190°C (375°F/gas mark 5).

Brush the muslin squares with oil and spread them flat on a board. Place equal numbers of bay leaves on each square, then place a pheasant on top, skin side down. Season the bird and fill it with the stuffing. Roll the pheasants up in the muslin, securing each tightly with string to form a Christmas cracker shape. Place these side by side in a large roasting tin and season the outside of the muslin with salt and pepper.

Roast the pheasants for 40–50min, then add the Marsala and stock to the tin and continue to cook for a further 10–15min. Unwrap the muslin and check whether the bird is cooked. To do this, insert a skewer into the middle of the stuffing and leave it there for 30sec. If the skewer comes out piping hot and no pink juices run from the bird, it's cooked. Transfer the pheasant on to a carving board and cover it with foil.

Mix the arrowroot with a little water and blend it into the juices from the roast pheasant. Bring this gravy to the boil, season to taste and strain into a warm gravy boat. Carve the pheasant and serve.

Pomegranate and Lychee Brulée

SERVES 6

1 ripe pomegranate

3 tbsp grenadine syrup

18 lychees, peeled and deseeded

3 egg yolks

2 level tbsp caster sugar

475ml (^{3}/$_4$ pint/2^1/$_2$ cups) double cream

Pared zest of 2 lemons

1 stick of lemongrass, roughly chopped

170g (6oz/^{3}/$_4$ cup) caster sugar

Split open the pomegranates and scoop out the seeds, removing as much of the bitter membrane and pith as possible. Mix the fruit with the grenadine and lychees, then divide between six ramekin dishes.

Place the egg yolks and caster sugar in a heatproof bowl and mix until creamy. In a lipped pan, heat the double cream, lemon zest and lemongrass to scalding point but do not boil. Remove from the heat and cool for a few minutes. Pour on to the egg mixture and return to the rinsed-out saucepan. Cook the cream over a very low heat, stirring constantly, until it thickens, but does not boil. Remove from the heat and strain into a cold bowl. Cool for 30min.

When cool, pour the cream over the pomegranate in the ramekins, cover and refrigerate for 4 hours or overnight.

When the pomegranate creams are cold, sprinkle the top of each with a generous amount of sugar. Caramelize the sugar by placing ramekins under a very hot, pre-heated grill or by using a kitchen blowtorch. Leave the brulées to stand for a few minutes to let the caramel set, then serve.

Ham and Puy Lentil Soup

In some parts of the world, lentils are eaten in celebration of prosperity – so they're a fitting ingredient to use on New Year's Day. The small and wonderfully nutty French Puy lentils are perfect for this dish, but any type can be used – just check whether those you use require pre-soaking. This recipe can be heated and kept warm in a thermos for a short time if you are planning some outdoor pursuits.

SERVES 6

225g (8oz/2 cups) Puy lentils, soaked for 1 hour in cold water

1 large onion, finely chopped

2 sticks celery, sliced

2 tbsp extra virgin olive oil

2 cloves garlic, crushed

2 tbsp tomato purée

1.35ltr (2 pints/5¼ cups) vegetable stock

225g (8oz/1 cup) cooked ham, diced

225g (8oz/1 cup) chorizo sausage, thickly sliced

2 tbsp freshly chopped herbs, such as rosemary and parsley

Rinse the soaked lentils in plenty of cold running water, then leave to drain.

Pour the oil into a large casserole pot, add the onion and celery and cook until soft. Add the garlic, tomato purée and lentils, and cook for a further 2min. Add the stock, bring to the boil, cover and simmer for 30min.

Add the ham and sausage, and continue to cook for a further 10min, or until the lentils are soft. Stir the herbs into the lentils, and season to taste with salt and plenty of freshly ground black pepper. Serve very hot.

Warm Ruby Chard Salad

There are few winter salad leaves, but chard is one that survives the cold well.

SERVES 6

450g (1lb) ruby chard, washed and dried

4 slices of Italian-style bread, such as foccacia

5 tbsp extra virgin olive oil

4 cloves garlic, unpeeled

2–3 sprigs of fresh rosemary

2 shallots, finely chopped

2 tbsp red wine vinegar

110g (4oz/1 cup) Dolcelatte, diced

2 tsp capers, rinsed and chopped

110g (4oz/1 cup) black olives, stoned

Heat the oven to 180°C (350°F/gas mark 4).

Tear the ruby chard into bite-sized pieces and place in a large serving bowl.

Cut the bread into 5cm (2in) chunks and arrange in a single layer on a baking sheet. Drizzle with 1 tbsp of the olive oil, scatter the garlic and sprigs of rosemary on top and season with plenty of black pepper. Bake for 20min, or until the bread is toasted and the garlic is soft.

In the meantime, make the dressing. Sauté the shallots in the remaining oil for 2–3min, or until they're softened at the edges, but still crunchy. Add the vinegar, Dolcelatte, capers and olives to the pan and immediately pour the sizzling dressing over the salad leaves. Sprinkle the foccacia croutons on top, and serve.

Rich Venison Tourtière

Serves 6

900g (2lb) venison, diced and trimmed of fat and gristle

150ml ($^1/4$ pint/ $^5/8$ cup) red wine

1 onion, finely sliced

8 juniper berries, crushed

340g (12oz) plain flour

$^1/2$ tsp salt

110g (4oz/$^1/2$ cup) butter

55g (2oz/$^1/4$ cup) lard

6–8 tbsp cold water

1 egg

1 egg yolk

1 tbsp sunflower oil

2 shallots, finely chopped

1 tbsp flour

150ml ($^1/4$ pint/ $^5/8$ cup) beef stock

55g (2oz/$^1/2$ cup) dried cranberries

1 tbsp redcurrant jelly

1 bay leaf

2 sprigs sage

3 tbsp soured cream

1 tbsp chopped sage

Place the venison in a large bowl and add the red wine, onion and juniper berries, then season well with pepper. Marinate overnight in the refrigerator.

To make the pastry, sift the flour and salt into a large bowl. Rub the butter and lard into the flour until the mixture resembles fine breadcrumbs. Briefly beat together 6 tbsp water and the eggs, then work this into the flour, adding more liquid, to a maximum of 8 tbsp, if necessary, to form a dough.

Turn the dough on to a lightly floured board and knead until smooth. Separate out one-quarter of the dough, wrap both pieces in greaseproof paper and chill for 30min. Preheat the oven to 150°C (300°F/gas mark 2).

Remove the venison from the marinade and pat dry. Strain the marinade and set aside. Heat the oil in a large casserole pot and brown the meat, a few pieces at a time. Transfer to a plate, then add the shallots to the pot and cook over a very low heat for 5–7min, or until they begin to soften. Add the flour and stir briskly for 1min. Stir in the reserved marinade and stock, place the venison in the pot and bring to the boil. Add the cranberries, redcurrant jelly and herbs. Cover and cook for $1^1/2$ hours, or until the meat is tender. Transfer the meat to a bowl and set aside to cool. Reduce the remaining sauce to 150ml ($^1/4$ pint) by boiling it rapidly, then season, if necessary, with salt and pepper, stir into the meat and leave to cool. Discard the bay leaf and sage.

Meanwhile, roll out the larger piece of pastry into a thin round to line a 23cm (9in) spring-form tin. Roll out the smaller round to form a thin pie lid and use any trimmings to make leaf decorations.

Stir the soured cream and chopped sage into the venison, then spoon into the centre of the pie. Dampen the edges of the pastry and seal the lid on top. Decorate with the pastry leaves and brush the top with beaten egg.

Bake at 190°C (375°F/gas mark 5) for 30–35min, or until the pastry is golden brown and the filling piping hot. Serve hot or cold.

Clementine Caramel Creams

SERVES 6

110g (4oz/ ^{1}/2 cup) granulated sugar

10 tbsp hot water

6 clementines or mandarins, peeled and trimmed of as much pith as possible

300ml (^{1}/2 pint/1 ^{1}/4 cups) milk

12 sugar lumps

3 clementines, washed

1 bay leaf

2 tbsp powdered gelatine or 8 leaves of gelatine

300ml (^{1}/2 pint/1 ^{1}/4 cups) single cream

4 tbsp Grand Marnier or Cointreau

6 small bay leaves, to decorate

Place the granulated sugar in a small saucepan with 5 tbsp of the hot water. Heat gently until the sugar has completely dissolved, then bring to the boil over a medium heat until the syrup has turned a rich dark caramel (too light and it will be too sweet; too dark and it will taste burnt).

Immediately the caramel is dark enough, and using oven gloves, pour the remaining boiling water into the caramel – it will hiss and splutter, so take care. Return the caramel to the heat and bring it to the boil, stirring to ensure there are no lumps. Remove from the heat and leave to cool.

Break peeled clementines into segments and stir into the cooled caramel. Set aside until required.

Pour the milk into a saucepan. Rub the sugar lumps over the skins of the clementines to lift off as much zest as possible, then drop the sugar into the milk, together with the bay leaf, and heat until the sugar has dissolved and the milk has reached scalding point.

Soak the gelatine in 6 tbsp cold water for 3–4min, add to the hot milk and leave to dissolve, stirring occasionally. After 10min, strain the milk into a bowl and leave to cool.

When the milk is cool, add the cream and Grand Marnier, and pour the mixture into six ramekins. Cover and leave to set in the refrigerator for 2 hours.

Just before serving, spoon the clementine caramel sauce over the top of the creams and decorate each with a bay leaf.

TWELFTH NIGHT AND EPIPHANY

As the twelve days of Christmas finish on 6 January, the season of Epiphany begins, continuing as part of the Christian calendar for six weeks.

The first day of Epiphany celebrates the day that the three kings visited the infant Jesus and offered their gifts of gold, frankincense and myrrh. It is on this day that many Eastern churches, and particularly the Greek Orthodox, celebrate the giving of gifts in recognition of the three kings, accompanied of course by a feast.

The eve of Epiphany, or Twelfth Night, on 5 January is celebrated as the last day of the Christmas festivities, and this is still an important day in some countries. This occasion was celebrated with a cake: a plum cake containing a bean would be enjoyed on Twelfth Night, the finder of the bean being in charge of revelries on this last feast of the Christmas period.

This same tradition of cake is carried right through Europe; probably the most famous is the French Epiphany cake still popular in French patisseries today, made with pastry filled with almond cream and containing a little figurine representing one of the three kings.

EPIPHANY/TWELFTH NIGHT LUNCH OR SUPPER

Middle Eastern Meze:

Chickpea, Cashew and Aubergine Hummus

Lamb Kibbeh

Stuffed Sweet Red Peppers

Baked Stuffed Jackets

Melon and Orange Flower Water Salad

Tangerine Granita

Serve the meze with olives and Horseradish Tzatziki (see page 175), along with plenty of warmed pitta bread and raw vegetable batons to dip.

To complement the spices in this meal, serve a Pinot Gris from Alsace.

Chickpea, Cashew and Aubergine Hummus

1 large aubergine

3 cloves garlic

150ml (1/4 pint/ 5/8 cup) extra virgin olive oil

340g (12oz/2 cups) cooked chickpeas

1–2 tbsp tahini (sesame seed paste)

Juice of 1–2 lemons

1 tsp cayenne pepper

2–3 tbsp chopped coriander

55g (2oz/1/2 cup) salted cashew nuts, roughly chopped

Olive oil and cayenne pepper, to garnish

To serve:

Warm pitta bread

Raw vegetable batons such as carrot, celery and cucumber

Heat the oven to 190°C (375°F/gas mark 5).

Pierce the aubergine with a sharp knife, then brush it and the garlic with a little of the olive oil. Arrange in a roasting tin and bake for 20min. Remove the garlic and continue to roast the aubergine for a further 20–25min, or until tender. Meanwhile, peel the garlic and set it aside. When the aubergine is cooked, peel it and place it in a sieve, pressing it hard to squeeze out as much juice as possible. Pat dry with absorbent paper.

Place the garlic, aubergine and chickpeas in a food processor, and whizz together to form a smooth purée. Add most of the remaining oil and the tahini and whizz again. Add the lemon juice and cayenne pepper to taste and season well with salt and pepper. Spoon the hummus into a bowl and stir in the coriander and cashew nuts, then transfer to a serving dish. Drizzle with a little more oil and sprinkle with a touch of cayenne pepper. Serve with the pitta bread and vegetable batons.

Lamb Kibbeh

MAKES 16

85g (3oz/³/₄ cup) bulghar wheat (cracked wheat)

Olive oil

¹/₂ tsp ground cinnamon

1 tsp ground cumin

1 tsp ground allspice

A pinch of cayenne pepper

1 red onion, very finely chopped

1 clove garlic, crushed

2–3 tbsp chopped mint

1 tbsp chopped parsley

225g (8oz) minced lamb

Lemon wedges and sprigs of coriander, to serve

Soak the bulghar wheat in boiling water for 10min, then drain and dry it on absorbent paper. Heat a splash of olive oil in a frying pan, add the bulghar wheat and the spices, and cook over a medium heat for 2–3min. Remove from the heat and leave to cool.

Place the spiced bulghar wheat in a food processor with the red onion, garlic and herbs, and whizz together until very well chopped. Transfer the mixture to a large bowl, add the minced lamb, and work the two together with your hands. Season very well with salt and pepper.

Heat the oven to 220°C (425°F/gas mark 7).

Shape the mixture into walnut-sized balls, then arrange them on a baking sheet and chill for 5–10min.

Bake the kibbeh in the oven for 10min, then reduce the temperature to 190°C (375°F/gas mark 5) and cook for a further 5min.

Remove from the oven and drain on absorbent paper. To serve, arrange the kibbeh on a platter and garnish with lemon wedges and sprigs of coriander.

Stuffed Sweet Red Peppers

SERVES 8

2 large red peppers

110g (4oz/1 cup) feta cheese, crumbled

55g (2oz/½ cup) fine breadcrumbs

12 green olives, stoned and chopped

Grated zest of ½ lemon

1 tbsp chopped parsley

1 tbsp capers

8 anchovy fillets

1 tbsp chopped oregano

2 tbsp extra virgin olive oil

Heat the oven to 150°C (300°F/gas mark 2).

Cut the red peppers in quarters and remove the inner pith and seeds. Place on a baking sheet, cut side uppermost, and season with plenty of freshly ground black pepper.

To make the filling, mix the feta cheese, breadcrumbs, olives, lemon zest, parsley and capers together, and season with salt, if necessary, and black pepper.

Spoon the filling into the peppers and arrange one or two anchovy fillets on each. Sprinkle the oregano over the top and drizzle with a little olive oil.

Bake for 1–1¼ hours, or until the peppers are soft. If they begin to blacken while cooking, cover them with aluminium foil.

Baked Stuffed Jackets

These baked potatoes can be prepared ahead of time – just ensure that all the other components are cold before assembling them for final baking.

SERVES 8

4 large baking potatoes

A little salt and oil

1 tbsp olive oil

1 small onion, finely diced

1 clove garlic, chopped

1 small aubergine, diced

1 tbsp tomato purée

1 red chilli, chopped

½ tsp ground coriander

2 chicken breasts, bones and skin removed

A pinch of nutmeg

200ml (7 fl oz/¾ cup) Greek yoghurt

2 egg yolks

55g (2oz/½ cup) soft goat's cheese, diced

Heat the oven to 190°C (375°F/gas mark 5).

Scrub the potatoes and prick them all over with a knife. Put a little salt and oil in the palm of your hand and rub all over the skins. Arrange potatoes on a baking sheet and bake for 1 hour, or until tender.

In the meantime, fry the onion in the oil for 5min. Add the garlic and the aubergine, cover the frying pan with a lid and sweat the vegetables over a very low heat for 10–15min. Remove the lid and stir in the tomato purée, chilli and coriander. Season to taste with salt and pepper.

Cut the chicken breasts into small cubes and add to the pan. Cover the pan again and cook the chicken over a low heat for 12–15min, or until just opaque – don't overcook it or it will be tough. Set aside and keep warm.

Cut the cooked potatoes in half and scoop the flesh into a bowl, taking care not to break the jackets. Season the potato flesh with salt and pepper, add the nutmeg and 2 tbsp of the Greek yoghurt and mash together with a fork. Turn the oven temperature down to 180°C (350°F/gas mark 4).

Arrange the jacket potatoes on a baking sheet and fill each three-quarters full with the mash, then top with the aubergine and chicken mixture, filling the jackets as generously as you can.

Mix the remaining Greek yoghurt with the egg yolk and cheese, then season with salt, freshly ground black pepper and a pinch of nutmeg. Spoon this mixture over the chicken filling. Bake for 20–25min, or until the yoghurt is set and the filling is piping hot, and serve.

Melon and Orange Flower Water Salad

SERVES 6

1 honeydew melon

1 small ogen melon

2 pink grapefruit

4–6 tbsp orange flower water

2–3 sprigs of mint, chopped

Icing sugar, to serve

Deseed the melons, remove the skin and cut into 4cm (1³/₄ in) chunks. Peel and separate the grapefruit into segments.

Place the fruit in a large serving bowl and sprinkle with the orange water. Cover with cling film and leave to infuse for 30–45min at room temperature.

To serve, sprinkle the mint over the top and dust generously with icing sugar, and spoon into glasses with the Tangerine Granita.

Tangerine Granita

SERVES 8

750ml (1¹/₄ pint/3¹/₃ cups) water

Pared zest and juice of 2 lemons and 6 tangerines or mandarins

225g (8oz/1 cup) granulated sugar

A few mint leaves (optional), plus extra to serve

Place the water, lemon and tangerine zest and granulated sugar in a large saucepan. Stir over a low heat until the sugar has dissolved, then bring to the boil and simmer for 5min.

Remove syrup from the heat, add the mint (if using) and leave to infuse for 30min. Strain the syrup and add the lemon and tangerine juice. Pour into a shallow plastic tray and freeze for 1 hour. Break the mixture into ice slush with a fork and continue to freeze for a further 2 hours or until completely frozen.

Half an hour before serving, remove the granita from the freezer and leave it to soften slightly in the refrigerator. Serve in chilled glasses, garnished with more mint leaves.

ST VALENTINE'S DAY

The feast of St Valentine on 14 February is one of the most commemorated feast days, since he is the patron saint of lovers all around the world. It has become commercialized, but is still a day for feasting in pairs! Valentine was martyred in the third century and it seems that his feast day on 14 February coincides with an old wives' tale that birds pair up on or around this day.

A dinner for two is the obvious celebration meal for this feast day, starting naturally with a dish of oysters. If you prefer an alternative, however, the same chilli dressing works well with smoked salmon or gravadlax – just remove the smoked fish from the refrigerator and its packing at least 30min before you plan to eat.

ST VALENTINE'S DAY DINNER FOR TWO

SERVES 2

Oysters with Sweet Chilli
and Mint

Calvados Guinea Fowl

Lemon Tabbouleh

Hot Mocha Truffle Soufflé

To complete this romantic dinner, serve a glass or two of Laurent Perrier rosé champagne.

Oysters with Sweet Chilli and Mint

When you buy the fresh oysters, ask your fishmonger to shuck (open) them. Always buy and eat oysters on the same day.

SERVES 2

For the dressing:

1 red chilli, deseeded and finely
chopped

2 tsp caster sugar

2 tsp rice wine vinegar

1 tsp chopped mint

Grated zest and squeeze of lime
juice

6 Pacific or Native oysters,
shucked

Mix all the ingredients for the dressing together.

Remove the top shell from the oysters and arrange them on a large plate of crushed ice. Spoon the dressing over the top and serve immediately.

Calvados Guinea Fowl

SERVES 2

2 tbsp sunflower oil

15g (½ oz/⅛ cup) butter

1 large Spanish onion, finely sliced

2 tsp flour

1 tsp dark brown sugar

2 sticks celery, finely diced

1 sweet potato, peeled and diced

1 large parsnip, peeled and thickly diced

Grated zest and juice of 1 lemon

1 small guinea fowl, cut into quarters

3 tbsp Calvados or brandy

150ml (¼ pint/⅝ cup) chicken stock

4 tbsp crème fraîche

1 tsp each chopped parsley and rosemary

Heat the oven to 170°C (325°F/gas mark 3).

Heat the oil and butter in a large casserole pot, add the onion and cook slowly until golden brown. Add the flour, sugar, celery, sweet potato, parsnip and lemon zest, and stir together over a low heat for 2–3min. Transfer the vegetables to a plate and set aside.

Brown the guinea fowl joints in the remaining oil in the casserole pot. Heat the Calvados, ignite and pour it, flaming, over the guinea fowl. Return the vegetables to the pot with the stock and bring to the boil. Season lightly with salt and black pepper. Cover and bake for 1–1¼hr, or until the meat is cooked.

Transfer the meat and vegetables to a plate. Skim off any fat from the cooking liquid in the pot and reduce it, if necessary, by boiling it rapidly. Add the crème fraîche, herbs and a little lemon juice, then season to taste with salt and freshly ground black pepper.

Return the guinea fowl and vegetables to the pot, mix with the reduced sauce and serve.

Lemon Tabbouleh

SERVES 2

110g (4oz/1 cup) bulghar wheat

225ml (8floz/1 cup) chicken stock

Grated zest and juice of 1 lemon

1 leek, finely sliced

2 tbsp pesto

Place the bulghar wheat in a sieve and rinse under cold running water for 30 seconds. Pour the stock into a saucepan and add the bulghar wheat, lemon zest and sliced leek. Bring to the boil and simmer for 4–5min. Remove from the heat and allow to stand for a few more minutes, or until the bulghar wheat is soft. Add the lemon juice and pesto, and season to taste with salt and black pepper. Reheat the tabbouleh over a low flame for 1–2min, stirring continuously, and serve.

Hot Mocha Truffle Soufflé

The Hot Mocha Truffle Soufflés can be made a few days in advance and frozen. They can then be baked straight from the freezer, but the cooking temperature should be increased to 200°C (400°F/gas mark 6) and they should be cooked for a further 5–7 min.

SERVES 2

A little melted butter

Caster sugar, to sprinkle

150ml (¼ pint/ ⅝ cup) milk

55g (2oz/½ cup) dark chocolate, grated

2 tsp cold strong coffee

2 tbsp caster sugar

½ tbsp flour

½ tbsp cornflour

3 eggs, separated

4 chocolate truffles, cut in half

Icing sugar, to dust

Heat the oven to 190°C (375°F/gas mark 5). Put a baking sheet on the top shelf of the oven. Brush two ramekins with the melted butter and sprinkle a little caster sugar on each.

Pour half of the milk into a small saucepan, add the chocolate and coffee, and stir over a very low heat until the chocolate has melted. Set aside to cool.

Put 1 tbsp of the sugar into a small bowl with the remaining milk, flour and cornflour, and beat together until the mix is creamy and light. Pour on the chocolate milk, stirring to blend, and return the mixture to the rinsed-out saucepan. Bring to the boil over a very low heat, stirring continuously, then simmer for 1min. Remove from the heat and leave to cool.

Place the egg whites in a clean, dry bowl and whisk until they form a stiff peak. Add the remaining caster sugar and continue to whisk for a further 30 seconds, until the whites look like satin. Stir the egg yolks into the mocha custard, then add the egg whites and fold in gently.

Spoon 3 tbsp of the soufflé mixture into each ramekin, place two truffles in the middle of each, then fill the ramekins to the top with the rest of the soufflé mixture. Use a knife to flatten the tops. Place the ramekins on the preheated baking sheet and bake for 12–14min, or until well risen, but still wobbly. Dust the soufflés with icing sugar and return them to the oven for 30 seconds. Serve immediately.

Spring Feasts

In ages past during February and March, when the winter had taken its toll, making the selection of produce limited, many foods were scarce and therefore meals were frugal. Today home-grown produce is still relatively scarce but plenty of foods imported from abroad fill the shelves. And in the garden we see the first hopeful anticipation of spring, as we begin to look forward to the coming year.

For the Church, the Christmas cycle finishes where the Easter cycle begins, seventy days before Easter Sunday. This time commemorates many of the important events during the adult life of Christ – his teaching, temptation, crucifixion and resurrection at Easter. It is the most important time of the year for the Church.

Easter is a moveable feast: its date changes each year to coincide with the Jewish feast of Passover, which is held soon after the first full moon after the spring equinox in March. The Passion of Christ, his betrayal, death and resurrection took place, according to the gospels, at the same time as the Jewish Passover, so it is remembered and celebrated at this time each year.

Before Easter, however, comes Lent. The time of Lent or Lenten, meaning lengthening days, was the first acknowledgement that spring was on the way. Yet the forty days of Lent also represent the time that Jesus spent fasting and praying in the wilderness, as documented in the gospels. Until fairly recently, rigid fasting was expected of church members during Lent. Several meals, including Friday night dinner and one or two breakfasts, were surrendered each week.

The period before Lent, or Shrovetide, was for the early Church a time of preparation before the strict rigours and sobriety of the Lenten fast. At the end of Shrovetide any prohibited foods, such as dairy produce, were used up, and so Shrove Tuesday has become the traditional day for pancake making.

The first day of Lent is Ash Wednesday. The name comes from the practice of anointing the brow with ashes, a reminder that from ashes we come and to ashes we will eventually return. Ash Wednesday is one of the holy days of obligation for members of the Catholic Church, when attendance of mass is essential.

During the forty days of Lent, there are several feast days to be remembered. In March we have two important feast days – the patron saint of Wales, St David, is celebrated on 1 March; the patron saint of Ireland, St Patrick, on the 17th. There is a mid-Lenten break for Mothering Sunday, on the fourth Sunday in Lent. It has more recently become the commercial Mother's Day, but was traditionally the day that people visited their mother church.

Holy Week, beginning with Palm Sunday and culminating on Easter Sunday, saw the end of Lent and the flourish of spring and a major celebration for the Church. On Palm Sunday we remember the occasion when Christ rode into Jerusalem on a donkey and a joyful crowd strewed his path with palms. Judas's betrayal of Christ to the Jewish authorities, on Wednesday of Holy Week, led to Wednesday being considered an important day of the week, one of penitence and fasting, during the course of the year.

The Last Supper on Maundy Thursday was also celebrated by various means round the country. The Last Supper, where Christ broke bread and offered wine, is symbolic for the Church as a representation of taking holy communion, when Jesus offers himself as the Passover lamb.

The Jewish festival of Passover celebrates the escape of the Jews from Egypt, led by Moses, as documented in Exodus. According to the Bible, the captive Jews were instructed to slaughter a year-old lamb and use some of its blood to mark their doors so that they would be protected from God's destruction of the Egyptians. Roast lamb thus became the centrepiece of the feast. The Passover lamb or kid is symbolic of God's protection for his people; it is served with bitter herbs, which are a reminder of their suffering in Egypt.

To commemorate the seven days of Passover, each house is spring-cleaned. No food containing a rising or leavening agent is allowed, especially yeast, but also various types of grain that also ferment – wheat, barley and rye are all forbidden foods. This represents the haste with which the Jews fled their homes in Egypt; there was no time to allow bread to rise.

Good Friday is the lowest point in the Christian calendar as it remembers the sacrifice of Christ at his crucifixion. The lamb, slaughtered as part of the Jewish Passover, has been adopted by the Christian Church as a symbol of the sacrifice of Christ. The high point in the calendar, Easter and the resurrection of Christ from the dead, is celebrated with joy and thankfulness in many countries around the world. It is a national holiday for many, as is the following Monday.

The Orthodox Eastern Catholic Church broke away from the Roman Church in the eleventh century and although they celebrate the same festivals, the dates of the moveable feasts differ. 'Greek' Easter is celebrated about two weeks later than the western churches; it usually falls in late April or even early in May. They have a traditional fast on Good Friday followed by a family gathering and festivities on Easter Sunday. It is recognized as being the most important day in their church calendar.

Remembering Christ's resurrection is only the start of the Easter celebrations. The story is completed during the time of the Ascension and Whitsunday.

St George's Day on 23 April is another important saint's feast day, on which the patron saint of England is celebrated.

May Day is the next holiday and by now we

realize that spring is really on the way. May Day was at one time a pagan festival celebrating the Celtic summer. Young saplings and flowers were gathered and dancing took place around a Maypole. A young woman was crowned Queen of the May in celebration of Flora, the Roman goddess of spring. Today's Morris dancers, bedecked with bells on their arms and legs, are believed by many to be reviving an ancient practice, and the entire day represents hopes of fertility for the coming summer.

SEASONAL INGREDIENTS IN SPRING

Homegrown produce is not yet abundant. On the vegetable front we still have the last of the winter roots and potatoes and onions are still in store from the previous summer.

Most of the produce available has weathered the winter, but it is worth looking out for new stocks of some spring vegetables as the earth begins to warm. Spring greens, spring onions and leeks are all available throughout March and April.

The early crop of new potatoes, and particularly the wonderful harvest of Jersey Royals, appears in late spring. The season for Jerseys is all too short, but they don't store well for any length of time, so you need to make the most of them when they appear in the shops. Asparagus appears in May, when it is at its least expensive, and it complements Jersey Royals to perfection in salads or as a hot vegetable.

Some types of fish are particularly good at this time of year. Costly but delicious, wild salmon comes into season in February, although it becomes more plentiful in summer. Many of the flat fish family are available: plaice, lemon sole and halibut are all at their best now. Mackerel and herrings are also very good.

Rhubarb, often considered a vegetable shoot and not a fruit at all, is good compensation for the lack of homegrown fruit. In the early part of spring, rhubarb is 'forced', grown under a terracotta cover which keeps out light; these shoots are a delicate pink and have a sharp but subtle flavour, perfect for mousses, crumbles and ice cream. Once the shoots become darker red in colour, the flavour is more pronounced; combined with preserved ginger it is perfect for preserves, or even as accompaniment to rich savoury, meat dishes.

We have lots to celebrate in spring, so I hope you enjoy the season of Lent and Easter.

Carrot and Hazelnut Cake

This cake is deliciously moist and rich, but is quite simple to make.

150ml (¼ pint/⅝ cup) sunflower oil

225g (8oz/1⅛ cup) soft brown sugar

4 eggs, beaten

2 tsp mixed spice

250g (9oz/2 scant cups) plain flour

2 tsp baking powder

85g (3oz/¾ cup) carrots, peeled and grated

85g (3oz/¾ cup) parsnip, peeled and grated

Grated zest and juice of ½ lemon

85g (3oz/ ¾ cup) toasted hazelnuts, ground

85g (3oz/ ¾ cup) fresh white breadcrumbs

For the marzipan:

225g (8oz/2 cups) toasted hazelnuts, ground

110g (4oz/⅝ cup) icing sugar

2 egg whites

For the lemon butter:

Grated zest and juice of 1 large lemon

170g (6oz/¾ cup) butter

225g (8oz/2 cups) icing sugar

Crystallized Primroses to decorate

Heat the oven to 180°C (350°F/gas mark 4).

Lightly oil a 25cm (10in) spring-form tin and line the base with non-stick baking parchment.

Place the oil, sugar and eggs in a bowl and whisk together for a few minutes until the sugar no longer feels gritty.

In a separate bowl, sift the mixed spice, flour and baking powder together, then add to the egg mixture, with the grated vegetables, lemon zest and juice, ground hazelnuts and breadcrumbs. Fold in until the ingredients are well combined.

Pour the mixture into the prepared tin and bake in the centre of the oven for 30–40min, or until a skewer inserted into the middle comes out clean. Leave the cake to cool in the tin for 5min. Loosen around the edges of the cake with a round-bladed knife, then remove from the tin and leave to cool on a wire rack.

To make the marzipan, mix the hazelnuts and icing sugar together. Add just enough egg white to draw the dry ingredients into a spreadable paste.

To make the lemon butter, cream the lemon zest, juice, butter and icing sugar together until light and fluffy.

Split the cake in half with a bread knife and spread the marzipan across the lower half. Replace the top half and arrange the cake on a 30cm (12in) cake board or plate. Spread the lemon butter over the top and sides of the cake with a palette knife, then arrange the crystallized primroses around the edge.

Crystallized Primroses

Many flowers lend themselves to being crystallized, but violets and rose petals are probably the most familiar. Take care to choose flowers that are not poisonous – as a general rule those grown from bulbs should not be used. Choose flowers that have only just opened and are not bruised in any way.

225g (8oz/1 cup) granulated sugar

5 tbsp boiling water

1–2 tbsp rose water (optional)

Primrose heads

Place the sugar and water in a saucepan over a low heat and stir until the sugar is completely dissolved. Bring the syrup to a fast boil and add the rose water. Simmer for 5min.

Remove the stalks from the primroses and drop them into the syrup. Bring to the boil, then reduce the heat and poach them for 1min.

Transfer the primrose heads to a piece of non-stick baking parchment and leave at room temperature for a day or so to harden. They can be stored in an airtight container for a few weeks.

SHROVE TUESDAY

Shrovetide was a time to prepare oneself for Lent, but it was also when all meat, poultry and dairy produce had to be used up before Lent began. It is from this custom that we have adopted the practice of pancake making on Shrove Tuesday. The making of pancakes represents the excitement of the coming of spring and the lengthening days to the spring equinox in March. Pancake races, in which the golden, sun-like pancake would be tossed over and over into the air, were held in recognition of the excitement of the sun rising higher and higher in the sky.

The opportunity to over-indulge and empty the store cupboard just before Lent gave rise to days such as Bursting Saturday, Bacon and Egg Sunday and Collop Monday, which all preceded Shrove Tuesday – these days were celebrated by various activities, fun and games around the country, but most importantly by feasting.

Carnival, a pagan time for feasting, took place across Europe during the first part of February; the last day being Shrove (derived from the word shrive, or absolve) Tuesday, a time to make confession before the abstinence of Lent. The Latin American celebrations of Carnival and Mardi Gras take place at this time.

This section includes a recipe for basic pancake batter, and two recipes for savoury and sweet fillings, which could be combined to make a simple supper, if you serve a few vegetables with the main course.

The following ideas make delicious sweet toppings, if you prefer to restrict your pancakes to a dessert: lemon juice and sugar; maple syrup and toasted pecan nuts; crème fraîche and lemon curd; blueberries and cream.

Pancake Batter

A really good pancake should be light, lacy and, strictly speaking, too delicate to toss. The secret of good pancakes, or crêpes, is a smooth batter about the thickness of single cream and a frying pan heated to the correct temperature. Don't worry if the first one doesn't work well; it rarely does. An old tradition was for an unmarried woman to give her first pancake to the cockerel – usually the best place for it!

Pancakes can be made and stored for up to a month in the freezer. Stack them between sheets of greaseproof paper and pack into a heavy-duty freezer bag.

TO MAKE 24 PANCAKES IN A 15CM (6IN) PAN

225g (8oz/1³/₈ cups) plain flour

A pinch of salt

2 whole eggs

2 egg yolks

300ml (¹/₂ pint/1¹/₄ cups) milk

300ml (¹/₂ pint/1¹/₄ cups) water

1 tbsp sunflower oil

To prepare the frying pan: If you have a cast iron frying pan or crêpe pan, add 1 tbsp oil and 1 tsp salt to it and heat. When the pan is very hot, rub the salt and oil around it. This will help to loosen and remove any sediment on the surface. Wipe the pan clean, but don't wash it. When you're ready to cook, lightly oil it. If you have a non-stick pan, just rub some oil around the base before cooking.

Sift the flour and salt together into a bowl. Make a well in the centre and add the eggs and a splash of the milk. Stir the liquid, so that the flour is gradually incorporated from the edges. As the mixture begins to thicken, add the remaining milk, water and oil and stir until the batter is the consistency of single cream. Cover and refrigerate for at least 15min.

Heat the prepared frying pan, but don't allow the oil to get too hot and smoke. Ladle in enough batter to just cover the base of the pan, then rapidly tip the batter around to form a thin coating. Leave the batter to cook for 1–2min, then loosen it from the base and flip it over with a palette knife. Cook for about 1min on the second side. Keep the cooked pancakes warm by stacking them on a plate over a pan of steaming water, covered with another plate.

Smoked Haddock, Swiss Chard and Gruyère Crêpes

SERVES 6

12 crêpes (pancakes)

450g (1lb) undyed smoked haddock, pinboned

300ml (½ pint/1¼ cup) milk

1 bay leaf

A piece of mace

A slice of onion

6 peppercorns

450g (1lb) Swiss chard, shredded

55g (2oz/¼ cup) butter

½ tsp ground coriander

2 level tbsp flour

½ tsp Dijon mustard

A pinch of cayenne pepper

110g (4oz/1 cup) Gruyère cheese, grated

For the topping:

30g (1oz/⅛ cup) melted butter

2 tbsp fine white breadcrumbs

Warm the crêpes on a plate placed over a saucepan of simmering water.

Put the haddock, skin side uppermost, into a large roasting tin. Pour the milk over the top and add the herbs, onion and peppercorns. Cover with a piece of greaseproof paper and poach over a very low heat for 8–10min, or until the fish is just cooked.

Remove the fish from the poaching liquid. Strain the cooking liquor and set aside. Remove the skin from the fish – it should peel away – and break the fish into large flakes.

Wash the chard in plenty of cold water, and dry. Heat half the butter and coriander in a large frying pan, and season with salt and pepper. Fry the chard, a handful at a time, over brisk heat for 2–3min, or until wilted and soft. Transfer to a plate.

Heat the oven to 190ºC (375ºF/gas mark 5).

To make the sauce, melt the remaining butter in a saucepan, add the flour, mustard and cayenne pepper, and cook over a low heat for 1min. Pour on the fish cooking liquor, stirring briskly to blend in the flour. Bring back to the boil and simmer for 2–3min. Add the chard, smoked haddock and half of the cheese, and season to taste.

Lay the crêpes on a large work surface, divide the mixture between the crêpes, and fold each one in half. Arrange the crêpes in a large gratin dish, sprinkle the remaining cheese on top and spoon over the melted butter and breadcrumbs. Bake until the crêpes are very hot and the gratin crust is lightly browned. Serve immediately.

Pear and Calvados Crêpes

SERVES 6

12 crêpes

6 ripe pears, peeled and diced

150ml (¼ pint/⅝ cup) apple juice

150ml (¼ pint/⅝ cup) water

1 tbsp granulated sugar

300ml (½ pint/1¼ cups) fromage frais

85g (3oz/⅜ cup) butter

1 tbsp light brown sugar

Grated zest of 1 lemon

A squeeze of lemon juice

4 tbsp Calvados or brandy

Warm the crêpes on a plate placed over a saucepan of simmering water.

Place the pears, apple juice, water and granulated sugar into a large saucepan. Bring to the boil and poach over a low heat for 15–20min, or until the fruit is tender. Remove the fruit and reduce the poaching liquid to 150ml (¼ pint/⅝ cup) by boiling rapidly. Pour the syrup over the pears and leave to stand for 5min. Place the crêpes on a clean work surface and put a spoonful of the fromage frais on to each. Divide the pear mixture between the crêpes and fold each into four.

Melt the butter in a large frying pan, add the sugar, lemon zest and juice and cook for 1–2min. Arrange the crêpe triangles in the hot sauce and spoon a little sauce over each.

Heat the Calvados in a ladle, ignite it and pour it, flaming, over the crêpes. Serve as soon as the flames have died down.

LENT

Forty days of fasting and praying in the wilderness were a time of reflection and preparation for Christ before his ministry, and symbolic of the forty years the Jews spent in the wilderness.

In days gone by the Church enforced strict dietary regulations on its members during Lent. Fasting for a complete forty days was not suggested, but certain restrictions were laid down. No dairy products, meat or poultry could be consumed during this time, with the exception of the family gathering on Mothering Sunday.

These restrictions caused quite severe hardship for the poorer communities, as their staples were meat, cheese and bread. Unless you lived within reach of the sea or a well-stocked river, suitable foods where in short supply. Lack of refrigeration meant that fish was often salted or dried. Pre-Reformation monasteries kept well-stocked ponds full of carp and other coarse fish, which provided an essential source of food. Various coarse fish which are sported more for pleasure than food today, including tench, perch, pike, even minnows, were all important.

The wealthy managed to work around the restrictions by stretching the rules somewhat. Although they could afford the fish that was on offer, it is suggested that sea birds, including puffin and gulls, became a popular dish during Lent. The gamey flavour of such birds was a welcome substitute for meat, but was arguably considered to be fish – as this was its staple diet!

Today Lent is often a forgotten time, or an opportunity to 'give something up' for a few days: chocolate, wine etc., anything considered to be a luxury. It might also be a time for our own personal reflection, and perhaps to consider a healthier diet in preparation for the warmer months ahead.

LENTEN FEASTS

The following recipes are ideal for lunches or informal suppers during the forty days of Lent.

Sweet Potato and Cardamom Soup

SERVES 4

450g (1lb/3 cups) sweet potatoes, peeled and diced

1 large potato (approximately 340g (12oz)), peeled and diced

2 cloves of garlic, chopped

1 bay leaf

Grated zest of 1 lime

1ltr (1¾ pint/4 cups) well-flavoured vegetable stock

8 cardamom pods, split and tied in a small piece of muslin

4 spring onions, thickly sliced

1 tbsp chopped coriander

Put all the potatoes into a large saucepan. Add the garlic, bay leaf, lime zest and stock, bring to the boil, add the cardamom and season with salt and pepper. Simmer for 25–30min or until the potatoes are tender.

Remove the cardamom and bay leaf. Transfer the cooked potatoes and stock to a liquidizer and whizz to form a smooth purée. Return the purée to the rinsed-out saucepan, adjust the seasoning and add a splash more stock if it's too thick. Add the spring onions, bring the soup back to the boil and simmer for 2–3min. Stir in the coriander, and serve with Oat and Sunflower Bread Rolls (see page 98).

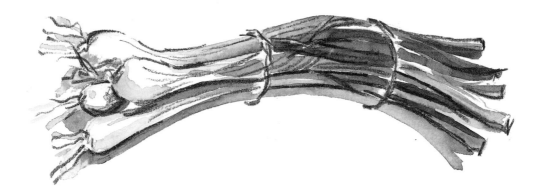

Oat and Sunflower Bread Rolls

MAKES 12

170g (6oz/1 cup) wholemeal flour

55g (2oz/⅓ cup) rye flour

225g (8oz/1⅓ cups) strong plain flour

1 heaped tsp salt

110g (4oz/1 cup) rolled oats

1 tbsp fresh yeast (or 2 tsp dried yeast)

1 tbsp runny honey

1 tbsp sunflower oil

300–425ml (½–¾ pint/1¼–1½ cups) warm water

2 tbsp sunflower seeds, toasted

Sift the flours and salt together into a large bowl. Stir in the oats.

Mix the yeast, 1 tsp of the honey and the sunflower oil together to form a smooth paste. Make a well in the centre of the flour, and add the yeast paste and two-thirds of the water. Stir the liquid, gradually incorporating the flour and adding more water if necessary to bring the mixture to a soft, but not sticky, dough.

Turn the dough on to a lightly floured surface and knead for 10–12min, or until smooth and elastic. Return the dough to a lightly oiled bowl. Cover it with a clean cloth and leave it to rise in a warm place for 1 hour, or until doubled in size.

Preheat the oven to 220°C (425°F/gas mark 7).

Place the risen dough on a board and knead it lightly to disperse any large air pockets. Divide the dough into twelve balls and shape each into a neat roll. Arrange on a lightly oiled baking tray, cover with a clean cloth and leave to 'prove' (rise a second time) for 10–15min.

Bake the rolls on the top shelf of the oven for 10min, then reduce the temperature to 190°C (375°F/gas mark 5) and continue to bake for a further 15–20min, or until they sound hollow when tapped on the underside. Transfer to a wire rack.

Warm the honey and brush over the hot rolls. Sprinkle with the sunflower seeds and leave the rolls to cool.

Smoked Haddock, Chilli and Chive Risotto

SERVES 4

225g (8oz) undyed smoked haddock

110g (4oz) haddock fillet

425ml (³⁄₄ pint/1³⁄₄ cups) skimmed milk

1 bay leaf

1 tbsp extra virgin olive oil

2 small leek, sliced

2 red chilli, deseeded and chopped

1 clove garlic, chopped

340g (12oz/2 cups) Arborio or Carnaroli risotto rice

900ml (1¹⁄₂ pint/3³⁄₄ cups) well-flavoured vegetable stock

1 medium carrot, peeled and thinly sliced

3 tbsp chopped chives

55g (2oz/¹⁄₂ cup) cooked peas

Place the haddock fillets in a large saucepan, pour over the milk and add the bay leaf. Poach the fish over a low heat for 10–12min or until just cooked. Skin the fish and remove any bones, then break the flesh into large flakes. Reserve the cooking liquor and discard the bay leaf.

Heat the oil in a large casserole and add the leek, chilli and garlic. Cook over a very low heat for 4–5min, stirring continuously. Stir the rice into the leek and continue to cook for a further 1min, taking care that the vegetables don't burn.

Heat the stock in a separate pan with the fish cooking liquor. Pour half of this fish stock over the rice and season it lightly with pepper. Add the carrot, cover the casserole and cook the rice over a low heat for 7–10min, stirring occasionally. Once the stock has been absorbed, add the remaining half. Cover and continue to cook until the rice is soft and the liquid absorbed. If any liquid remains once the rice is cooked, stir the risotto over a brisk heat to allow evaporation. Add the cooked fish to the risotto and heat through well. Adjust the seasoning and add the chives and peas just before serving. Serve with green salad leaves.

Slow-baked Pulse Stew

SERVES 4

450g (1lb) tinned cooked beans in
total, such as:

110g (4oz/ 1 cup) aduki beans

110g (4oz/1 cup) cannellini beans

110g (4oz/1 cup) haricot beans

110g (4oz/1 cup) red kidney beans

55g (2oz/^{1}/2 cup) dried Puy lentils

1 large onion, finely chopped

2 cloves garlic, crushed

1 carrot, peeled and finely diced

2 sticks celery, finely diced

600ml (1 pint/2^1/2 cups) V8 or
carrot juice

600ml (1 pint/2^1/2 cups) vegetable
stock

2 tbsp Worcestershire sauce
(optional for vegetarians)

2 tbsp tomato purée

2 tbsp muscovado sugar or
molasses

1 tbsp Dijon mustard

15g (^{1}/2oz/^{1}/8 cup) dried porcini
mushrooms, soaked in boiling
water for 5min

2 tbsp freshly chopped herbs, such
as sage, rosemary and parsley

Heat the oven to 140ºC (275ºF/gas mark 1).

Rinse the tinned beans under cold running water and
tip them into a large casserole dish. Add the Puy lentils,
onion, garlic, carrot, celery, vegetable juice and stock.
Bring to the boil and add the Worcestershire sauce, if
using, and the tomato purée, sugar and mustard.
Season lightly with salt and pepper. Cover and stew for
2 hours, checking the beans during the cooking – if they
begin to dry out add a little more water.

Add the porcini mushrooms and continue to cook
for a further 30min.

Adjust the seasoning, stir in the herbs, and serve with
Oat and Sunflower Bread Rolls (see page 98).

Root Vegetable and Seafood Casserole

SERVES 4

1 leek, thinly sliced

1 large potato, peeled and diced

1 parsnip, peeled and diced

2 carrots, peeled and thinly sliced

1ltr (1³/₄ pints/4 cups) fish stock

225g (8oz/1 cup) tinned tomatoes

225g (8oz/1 cup) soaked and cooked chickpeas

1 tbsp honey

1 bay leaf

2 sprigs of rosemary

450g (1lb) live mussels, scrubbed and de-bearded

2 trout fillets, skinned and cut into strips

170g (6oz) pollack, coley or cod fillet, skinned and cut into strips

2 plaice fillets, skinned and cut into strips

2 tbsp flour

¹/₂ tsp cayenne pepper

¹/₂ tsp ground ginger

¹/₂ tsp ground coriander

2 tbsp finely chopped parsley

Place all the vegetables in a large saucepan with the stock, tinned tomatoes, chickpeas, honey and herbs. Bring to the boil and simmer over a very low heat for 15–20min, or until the vegetables are just tender.

Check that the mussels are alive – the shells should be tightly shut and undamaged – and discard any that feel particularly heavy or that won't shut when sharply tapped.

Put the prepared fish on to a large tray. Mix together the flour and spices, and season generously with salt and pepper. Roll each piece of fish in the flour until well coated.

Add the mussels to the cooked vegetables. Bring the casserole back to the boil, cover the pot and poach the mussels over a low heat for 2–3min. Add the coated fish and poach for a further 4–5min, or until the mussel shells are open and the fish is cooked. Discard any mussels that haven't opened. Adjust the seasoning, sprinkle the parsley on top and serve with pasta or bread.

Sea-bass and Oriental Noodle Envelopes

If sea-bass is unavailable, use any small fillet of fish instead.

SERVES 4

4 x 170g (6oz) fillets of sea-bass, skinned and pinboned

2 tbsp sesame oil

340g (12oz/3 cups) egg noodles, cooked and drained

200g (7oz/1 cup) tinned water chestnuts, thickly sliced

200g (7oz/1 cup) tinned bamboo shoots, drained

4 spring onions, finely sliced

1 red chilli, deseeded and finely chopped

4 tbsp dark soy sauce

Brush the sea-bass fillets with the sesame oil, season with black pepper and set aside.

Place the egg noodles in a large bowl, add the vegetables, chilli and soy sauce, season well with salt and pepper, and toss together.

Cut four 30cm (12in) squares of aluminium foil and the same of non-stick baking parchment. Place a paper square on top of each foil square. Divide the noodles between the four squares, then arrange a fillet of fish on top and fold the paper and foil to close the envelope. Pinch and twist the edges of the foil together to make a secure package. Chill until required.

Heat the oven to 220°C (425°F/gas mark 7).

Put a baking sheet in the oven to heat. Place the envelopes on to the pre-heated baking sheet and bake for 18–20min, or until the fish is cooked and the noodles are very hot.

Loosen the envelope edges slightly, and serve immediately with a selection of sliced vegetables stir-fried in sesame oil.

Gremolata Cod
with Braised Leeks and Olives

SERVES 4

4 x 170g (6oz) cod steaks

2 tsp fresh thyme, chopped

1 tbsp chopped parsley

1 clove garlic, finely chopped

Grated zest of 1 lemon

2 tbsp olive oil

6 leeks, thickly sliced and washed

5 tbsp fish stock

110g (4oz/$\frac{1}{2}$ cup) green olives, pitted and halved

Heat the oven to 180°C (350°F/gas mark 4).

Place the cod on a plate and season with salt and pepper. Mix together the herbs, garlic and lemon zest, sprinkle over the fish and set aside.

Heat the oil in a casserole dish, and stir-fry the leeks over a medium heat for 3–4min. Add the stock and olives, and season lightly with salt and pepper.

Arrange the cod on top of the leeks, cover the casserole and bake for 15–18min, or until the fish is cooked and the leeks are soft.

Serve with plenty of mashed potatoes.

Grilled Sole with Wilted Spinach

SERVES 4

4 double fillets of Dover or lemon sole

1 tbsp rock salt

A pinch of cayenne pepper

Sunflower oil

1 tbsp flavoured oil, such as garlic, chilli or basil

4 spring onions, finely sliced

450g (1lb) spinach or sorrel, if available

A pinch of grated nutmeg

Grated zest of 1 lemon

1 lemon, cut into wedges, to serve

Make 3–4 diagonal slashes across the skin and into the flesh of each fish fillet. Mix the salt, cayenne pepper and oil together, and rub the mixture over the skin and into the cuts. Set aside to marinate for 10min.

Heat the grill to its highest setting and grill the fish, skin side up, for 4–5min, or until the skin comes loose and the fish has lost its translucency.

In the meantime, prepare the spinach. Heat the oil in a large frying pan until it's very hot, add the spring onions and spinach and cook over a very high heat for 2–3min until the spinach is wilted. Add the nutmeg, lemon zest and season to taste with salt and pepper.

Divide the wilted spinach between four warmed dinner plates and arrange the fish on top, skin side uppermost. Garnish with wedges of lemon and serve immediately with baked or new potatoes, if available.

Roast Allium Salad with Warm Onion Seed Dressing

Members of the allium family include onions, leeks, chives and garlic, most of which are available all year round. They play an essential part in thousands of dishes from around the world and are credited with many health benefits, too.

SERVES 4

1 large Spanish onion, peeled and cut into 8 wedges

2 cloves garlic, unpeeled

6 shallots, peeled and cut in half

2 leeks, thickly sliced

4 sprigs of rosemary

2 tbsp olive oil

Plenty of bitter leaves, including frisée, chicory or radicchio

3 tbsp olive oil

1 red onion, finely chopped

2 tbsp onion seeds (kaljoni)

1 tbsp sherry or red wine vinegar

1 tbsp chopped chives

Heat the oven to 190°C (375°F/gas mark 5).

Place the onions, garlic, shallots and leeks in a large roasting tin. Scatter the rosemary on top and drizzle with the oil. Season with salt and pepper.

Roast for 20min, then remove the garlic cloves and set aside. Roast the other vegetables for a further 20min, then remove the leeks. Roast the onions and shallots for another 10–15min or until tender and well browned.

Divide the salad leaves between four plates and arrange the warm vegetables on top.

Heat the oil in a frying pan and cook the red onion and onion seeds over a medium heat for 1–2min. Season with salt and pepper. Add the vinegar and chives and, while still sizzling, pour the dressing over the roast alliums. Serve immediately with ciabatta or naan bread.

Spiced Mango, Pineapple and Orange Compôte

SERVES 4

300ml (¹/₂ pint/1¹/₄ cups) orange juice

1 vanilla pod

2 whole cloves

6 black peppercorns

55g (2oz/¹/₂ cup) dried mango, thinly sliced

5cm (2in) piece root ginger, peeled and very finely sliced

Pared zest of 2 oranges, finely shredded

1 ripe mango, peeled and thickly sliced

1 ripe pineapple, peeled and thickly sliced

2 oranges, segmented

1 tbsp roughly chopped mint

Place the orange juice, vanilla pod, cloves and peppercorns in a saucepan, bring to the boil, remove from the heat and leave to infuse for 30min.

Strain the infused juice and return it to the saucepan with the dried mango, ginger and orange zest. Poach the fruit on a very low heat for 5min, then leave to cool.

Place the fresh mango, pineapple and orange segments in a large serving bowl. Add the juice and sprinkle the chopped mint over the top. Serve the compôte warm, with natural yoghurt.

MOTHERING SUNDAY

The fourth Sunday in Lent is Mothering Sunday, which was an opportunity to take a break from the rigours of the strict dietary restrictions of Lent. The original day was nominated for people to visit their 'mother' church.

Later Mothering Sunday became the day that girls in service would take a day's holiday and visit their own mother, and it was on this day that recipes for Simnel cake came about. Simnel cake is often regarded as an Easter cake but there were many recipes that preceded it. Today it is a rich fruit cake with a layer of marzipan through the middle and on top. The decorations are eleven balls of marzipan – to represent eleven of the disciples, minus Judas – with one in the centre to represent Jesus.

In many counties across Britain there are traditional recipes to celebrate this feast day. There are recipes for roasted veal, young lamb or pork, all celebrating the beginning of spring.

This is a great day for a fabulous family tea.

MOTHERING SUNDAY TEA

Tropical Fruit Scones
Pineapple and Lime Jam
Honey and Hazelnut Loaf
Sticky Chocolate Fudge Fingers

Tropical Fruit Scones

MAKES 10

340g (12oz/2 cups) self-raising flour

½ tsp baking powder

85g (3oz/³⁄₈ cup) butter, chilled and cubed

110g (4oz/²⁄₃ cup) dried mango, papaya or pineapple, roughly chopped

150–200ml (5–7fl oz/⁵⁄₈–⁷⁄₈ cup) milk

2 tbsp double cream

Flour, to dust

Heat the oven to 190°C (375°F/gas mark 5). Dust a baking sheet with a little flour.

Sift the flour and baking powder into a large bowl. Add the butter and rub it into the flour until the mixture resembles fine breadcrumbs. Stir in the dried fruit.

Mix the milk and cream together, then add just enough to the flour to form a soft, but not sticky, dough.

Turn the dough on to a lightly floured baking sheet and shape it into a round, 20cm (8in) in diameter, with your fingers. Mark out 10 wedges with the back of a knife, dust the top with a little flour.

Bake for 30–35min or until well risen and golden brown, then transfer to a wire rack to cool.

Cut into wedges and serve with jam, such as Pineapple and Lime (see page 108), and mascarpone cheese.

Pineapple and Lime Jam

Take care to choose pineapples that are only just ripe – if they're beginning to over-ripen, the jam will either not set well or will turn mouldy very quickly.

MAKES 2.3KG (5LBS)

2 large pineapples, peeled and diced (cores removed)

450g (1lb/2 cups) preserving sugar for every 450g (1lb/3 cups) pineapple

Grated zest and juice of 8 limes

Jam jars and covers

To sterilize the jam jars, heat the oven to 100°C (200°F/gas mark $^{1}/_{2}$). Wash jars in hot soapy water and put to dry, upside down on a tray, in the oven.

Put the pineapple and any of its juice into a large saucepan or preserving pan. Add the sugar and grated lime zest. Heat very gently until the sugar has dissolved, then bring to the boil and simmer very gently for 45–50min, or until the pineapple has turned glassy. Add the lime juice, bring the fruit back to the boil and simmer for 3–4min.

At this stage, test the jam to see if it has reached setting point – put a spoonful on to a cold plate and refrigerate for 5min. If a wrinkly skin forms, the jam is ready.

As soon as it reaches setting point, remove the jam from the heat and skim off any residue on the surface.

Leave the jam to cool slightly for 15min, then transfer it to a jug and pour it into the hot jars. Cover each with a wax disc and a dampened pot cover, securing this with an elastic band. Label and store in a cool place for up to six months.

Honey and Hazelnut Loaf

Use the Candied Citrus Peel (see page 51) here, or use ready-made, if you prefer.

110g (4oz/$^{1}/_{2}$ cup) butter

110g (4oz/$^{5}/_{8}$ cup) soft light brown sugar

2 large eggs, beaten

55g (2oz/$^{1}/_{3}$ cup) candied peel, chopped

110g (4oz/$^{1}/_{2}$ cup) skinned hazelnuts, toasted

140g (5oz/$^{1}/_{2}$ cup) runny honey

150ml ($^{1}/_{4}$ pint/$^{5}/_{8}$ cup) buttermilk

Grated zest of 1 small orange

225g (8oz/$1^{2}/_{3}$ cups) plain flour

1 level tsp bicarbonate of soda

Heat the oven to 150ºC (300ºF/gas mark 2). Lightly oil a 1.3ltr (2 pint/5 cups) loaf tin, put a strip of lightly oiled baking parchment down the centre and dust it with flour.

Cream the butter and sugar together until pale. Add the eggs, a little at a time, beating well between each addition. Stir in the candied peel, nuts, honey, buttermilk and orange zest. Sift the flour and bicarbonate of soda together into a large bowl, make a well in the centre and add the honey and fruit batter. Carefully stir the flour into the batter until smooth.

Pour the batter into the prepared tin and bake on a middle shelf for about 1 hour – the loaf is cooked when a skewer inserted into the middle comes out clean. Cover the loaf with aluminium foil while cooking if the top browns too quickly. Transfer to a wire rack to cool for 10min.

Serve the loaf still warm with butter curls or clotted cream.

Sticky Chocolate Fudge Fingers

MAKES 12

170g (6oz/³/4 cup) dark chocolate, chopped

85g (3oz/³/8 cup) unsalted butter

¹/2 tsp vanilla essence

55g (2oz/¹/3 cup) soft light brown sugar

3 eggs, separated

85g (3oz/¹/2 cup) ground rice

2 tsp caster sugar

for the icing:

30g (1oz/¹/8 cup) dark chocolate, chopped

2 tbsp water

1 tsp butter

110g (4oz/¹/2 cup) cream cheese

2–3 tbsp icing sugar

Milk and white chocolate buttons, to decorate

Heat the oven to 180ºC (350ºF/gas mark 4). Lightly oil an oblong, deep-sided baking tray measuring 15x25cm (6x10in). Line the base with non-stick baking parchment.

Place the chocolate, butter and vanilla essence in a heatproof glass bowl. Sit the bowl over a saucepan of simmering water (don't allow the water to touch the bowl). Stir until the chocolate has semi-melted, then remove from the heat and stir until the chocolate has melted completely. Put aside to cool but not harden.

Cream the brown sugar and egg yolks together until light and fluffy, then fold into the cooled chocolate mixture, with the ground rice.

Whisk the egg whites in a clean dry bowl until stiff peaks form. Add the caster sugar and whisk for a further 30 seconds. Fold the egg whites well into the chocolate mixture. Spoon the mixture into the prepared tin and bake on the middle shelf of the oven for 25–30min, or until a skewer inserted into the middle comes out sticky. The cake should be very moist when baked.

Leave the cake to cool in the tin for 10min, then transfer it to a wire rack to cool completely before icing.

To make the icing, melt the chocolate, water and butter together in a small bowl set over simmering water, taking care not to let it overheat. Allow it to cool again for 2min, then stir it into the cream cheese with the icing sugar. Spread the icing over the cake.

Cut the cake into fingers approximately 2.5x10cm (1x4in). Decorate each with chocolate buttons, and serve.

PALM SUNDAY

Palm Sunday, the Sunday before Easter Sunday, is the sixth Sunday in Lent and the beginning of Holy Week, and is a day to commemorate Christ's triumphal entry into Jerusalem. It is still traditional in many churches for members of the congregation to receive a cross, made from a dried palm leaf, to mark this day.

In many countries across Europe there are various traditional celebrations, but in England the day was once known as Fig Sunday. Dried figs, mainly used in a good old-fashioned fig pudding, represented the withered fig tree that Christ passed by on his ride into Jerusalem as recalled in St Mark's gospel.

Palm Sunday, like Easter, can fall in March or April, depending on the church calendar. Our menu for Palm Sunday is a family lunch and a representation of all the good things that spring has to offer.

PALM SUNDAY LUNCH

Charred Spring Chicken with Rosemary and Garlic
Parsnip Gratin
Ginger and Mascarpone Cake with Rhubarb Compôte
Marinated Sesame Seed Figs

To complete the menu, serve some steamed spring greens with the chicken and parsnips, and enjoy the figs with coffee. If you feel like a glass of wine, choose a stylish Italian red from Trentino.

Charred Spring Chicken
with Rosemary and Garlic

SERVES 4

4 chicken quarters

55g (2oz/¼ cup) butter

2 tbsp chopped rosemary

2 cloves garlic, peeled

Juice of 1 lime

2 tbsp soft dark brown sugar

A large pinch of paprika

150ml (¼ pint/⅝ cup) chicken stock

1–2 tsp arrowroot

Heat the oven to 200°C (400°F/gas mark 6).

Trim the chicken joints if necessary and arrange, skin side uppermost, in a roasting tin.

Mix the butter, rosemary, garlic, lime juice, sugar and paprika together, and season with salt and pepper. Spread this mixture over the chicken joints.

Bake for 15min, then baste with the cooking juices and bake for a further 15min.

Increase the oven temperature to 230°C (450°F/gas mark 8).

Baste the chicken joints again, then move them to the top shelf of the oven for a further 5min, or until the chicken is dark brown and the juices are reduced to a glaze. To check whether the chicken is cooked, pierce the meat and be sure the juices run clear, not pink.

Transfer the chicken to a serving dish. Pour the cooking juices into a jug, skim away the excess fat and pour the remaining juice into a saucepan. Add the chicken stock, bring to the boil and simmer for 1–2min.

Mix the arrowroot with a little water and stir it into the simmering liquid, then season with salt and pepper. Trim the chicken joints and arrange them on a large serving dish. Hand the gravy separately.

Parsnip Gratin

SERVES 4

2lb (900g) parsnips, peeled, cored and chopped

55g (2oz/¼ cup) butter

4–5 tbsp hot milk

½ tsp grated nutmeg

55g (2oz/½ cup) Parmesan cheese, grated

Heat either the grill or the oven on a high setting.

Cook the parsnips in boiling salted water for 12–15min, or until tender. Drain and toss them over the heat for 1–2min to dry.

Mash the parsnips and add the butter, milk, nutmeg and half of the cheese, and season to taste with salt and pepper.

Spoon into a dish and sprinkle with the remaining cheese. Brown the top of the gratin either under the grill or in a very hot oven.

Marinated Sesame Seed Figs

SERVES 6

225g (8 oz/1½ cups) semi-dried figs

2 tbsp runny honey

3 tbsp brandy

2 tbsp toasted sesame seeds

Soak the figs in the brandy for 4 hours.

Warm the honey in a small saucepan, then add the figs and roll them over a few times until completely coated. Transfer the figs to a plate and leave to cool.

Scatter the sesame seeds on a tray and toss the figs in the seeds until they're well coated. Serve the figs in petit four cases, with coffee.

Ginger and Mascarpone Cake with Rhubarb Compôte

SERVES 4–6

For the base:

225g (8oz/1 cup) ginger biscuits, crushed

55g (2oz/¹/4 cup) unsalted butter, melted

2 tbsp soft brown sugar

For the cake:

340g (12oz/1¹/4 cups) mascarpone cheese

125mls (4 fl oz/¹/2 cup) crème fraîche

3 eggs

1 egg yolk

4 pieces stem ginger, finely chopped

2 tbsp stem ginger syrup

For the compote:

5 tbsp stem ginger syrup

4 tbsp soft brown sugar

450g (1lb) rhubarb, thickly sliced

2 tbsp icing sugar

¹/2 tsp ground ginger, to dust

Heat the oven to 150°C (300°F/gas mark 2).

Place all the ingredients for the base in a bowl and mix thoroughly. Spoon into a 25cm (10in) flan ring, pressing it flat with the back of a spoon, and bake for 10min. Set aside to cool.

Place the ingredients for the cake into a bowl and beat until smooth. Pour the mixture over the ginger biscuit base and bake for 40–50min, or until the filling is set. Set aside to keep warm.

Place all the ingredients for the compôte in a medium-sized saucepan, cover and cook over a very low heat for 7–10min, or until the rhubarb is just tender, stirring every so often to prevent it from sticking. Lift the rhubarb out of the liquid with a slotted spoon and set aside in a bowl. Reduce the juice to a syrupy consistency by boiling it rapidly, then pour it over the rhubarb.

To serve: Mix the icing sugar and ginger together and sift over the top of the cake. Cut the cake into wedges, spoon a little compôte over the top and serve warm.

GOOD FRIDAY

Good Friday is the darkest and most sombre day in the Christian calendar as it commemorates the death of Christ, the Son of God, on the cross. Lenten food is usually the diet for this day, although some choose to fast completely during daylight hours, with only water and a little vinegar as sustenance. Good Friday diet is often associated, as with other Fridays during the year, with eating fish, which is usually salted and served with simply boiled vegetables.

Hot cross buns are traditional English fare for Good Friday. The cross on the top, made with a flour and water paste, represents the cross of Christ; it was also intended as a defence against the evil powers that surround us.

GOOD FRIDAY BREAKFAST OR TEA

Traditional Hot Cross Buns

GOOD FRIDAY SUPPER

SERVES 6

Cod, Scallop and Champ Pie
Poached Rhubarb with Zabaglione and Honey Tuiles

To complete the menu, serve the cod pie with steamed leeks and carrots.

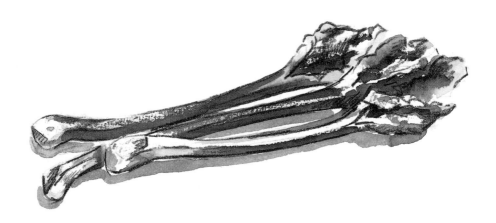

Traditional Hot Cross Buns

MAKES 15

675g (1½ lb/5 cups) strong plain flour

2 tsp ground cinnamon

1 tsp grated nutmeg

2 tsp mixed spice

1 level tsp salt

110g (4oz/½ cup) butter

1 tbsp fresh yeast, or 2 tsp dried yeast

85g (3oz/½ cup) soft dark brown sugar

250ml (8fl oz/1 cup) milk, approximately

2 eggs

2 tbsp raisins

3 tbsp currants

4 tbsp sultanas

4 tbsp plain flour

A pinch of bicarbonate of soda

Water, to mix

A little honey, to glaze

Sift the flour, spices and salt into a large bowl. Rub the butter into the flour until the mixture resembles fine breadcrumbs.

Mix the yeast and 2 tsp of the sugar together until a liquid forms. Warm the milk until tepid, then remove from the heat. Stir the yeast into the warm milk. Make a well in the centre of the flour and add the yeast/milk mix, eggs and remaining sugar. Combine to form a soft, but not sticky, dough.

Turn the dough on to a lightly floured board and knead it for 7–8min. Place it in a lightly oiled bowl, cover the bowl with oiled cling film and leave the dough to rise for 1 hour, or until doubled in bulk.

Heat the oven to 200ºC (400ºF/gas mark 6).

Turn the risen dough on to a lightly floured board and knead for a further 2–3min. Sprinkle the dried fruit over the top and knead the dough for a further 1–2min, until the fruit is mixed in well.

Divide the dough into 15 pieces. Shape each into a ball and cut a cross in the top, then arrange on a lightly oiled baking sheet. Cover with a clean cloth and leave to prove (rise a second time) for 10–12min.

Sift the flour and bicarbonate of soda together, and add just enough water to form a thick paste. Fill a piping bag, fitted with a 1cm (½in) plain nozzle, with the mixture and pipe along the cuts in each bun to form a cross.

Bake on the top shelf of the oven for 25–30min, or until well risen – the buns should sound hollow when tapped on the underside. Warm the honey in a saucepan and brush the top of each bun, while still warm, to glaze it. Leave the buns to cool on a wire rack.

Serve the Hot Cross Buns as they are or toasted and buttered.

Cod, Scallop and Champ Pie

SERVES 6

675g (1½lb) potatoes, peeled and cut into quarters

85g (3oz/⅜ cup) butter

A large bunch of spring onions, sliced

125ml (4fl oz/½ cup) hot milk

A little grated nutmeg

450g (1lb) cod fillet, skinned

225g (8oz) smoked cod, skinned

450ml (¾ pint) milk

1 bay leaf

55g (2oz/¼ cup) butter

1 leek, thinly sliced

110g (4oz) button mushrooms, thickly sliced

2 heaped tbsp flour

1x170g (6oz) jar cockles (optional)

110g (4oz) queen scallops

1 tbsp chopped parsley

Cook the potatoes in boiling salted water for 15–20min or until tender. Drain and push through a sieve, then return mash to the saucepan. Cover and set aside. Heat the butter in a saucepan and sauté the spring onions. Add to the potatoes, with the hot milk and stir to combine. Season to taste with salt, freshly ground black pepper and nutmeg, cover and set aside.

Place the cod and smoked cod in a large saucepan and add the milk and the bay leaf. Bring the milk to the boil, reduce the heat and poach the fish for 5–7min or until it's just cooked and looks opaque. Strain the cooking liquor off and reserve. Flake the fish and remove any bones, and set aside.

Heat the butter in a large saucepan and sauté the leek and mushrooms for 4–5min, or until soft. Add the flour and stir in briskly to form a paste, then cook over a low heat for 1–2min. Add the fish liquor a little at a time, blending into the flour to make a sauce, then bring to the boil, stirring continuously. Simmer for 1min, then add the cockles and scallops and cook for 30 seconds. Add the flaked fish and the chopped parsley, and season to taste.

Heat the oven to 190°C (375°F /gas mark 5). Transfer the fish mixture to a large pie dish and spread the potato champ on top with a fork. Put the dish on a baking sheet and bake for 25–30min or until the pie is very hot and the top is crusty and brown.

Poached Rhubarb with Zabaglione and Honey Tuiles

Tuiles are curved biscuits and are named after traditional French curved roof tiles.

SERVES 6

For the tuiles:

2 egg whites

55g (2oz/¼ cup) caster sugar

4 tbsp runny honey

55g (2oz/⅓ cup) plain flour

55g (2oz/⅛ cup) unsalted butter, melted

For the rhubarb:

450g (1lb) pale rhubarb

2–3 tbsp raspberry jam

Grated zest of 1 lemon

2–4 tbsp caster sugar

For the zabaglione:

4 egg yolks

55g (2oz/¼ cup) caster sugar

4 tbsp Amontillado sherry

Juice of ½ lemon

55g (2oz/¼ cup) toasted flaked almonds, to serve

Heat the oven to 170°C (325°F/gas mark 3).

To make the tuiles, whisk the egg whites in a clean dry bowl until they form stiff peaks. Add the caster sugar a little at a time, whisking well between each addition. Add the honey and stir in lightly.

Sift the flour into the mixture and add the cold butter, stirring until the mix becomes like a paste.

Put spoonfuls of the mixture on to a baking sheet, lined with non-stick baking parchment, and spread into thin rounds with the back of a teaspoon. Bake on the middle shelf of the oven for 5–7min, or until a very pale golden brown.

Remove from the oven and leave to cool on the baking sheet for 2–3min, then remove from the paper with a palette knife and shape into curls over a lightly oiled rolling pin. Leave to cool.

Cut the rhubarb into 2.5cm (1in) lengths. Place in a saucepan with 2 tbsp of the raspberry jam, the lemon juice and 2 tbsp of the caster sugar. Cook over a very low heat for 5–6min, or until the fruit is tender. Taste and add more jam or sugar as required, then set aside to keep warm.

To make the zabaglione, place the egg yolks, sugar, sherry and lemon juice in a glass bowl set over, rather than in, a saucepan of simmering water. Whisk until the mixture becomes very pale and frothy.

Divide the warm rhubarb between six large wine glasses and spoon the zabaglione on top, then sprinkle with the almonds. Serve immediately, with the tuiles.

EASTER SUNDAY

Easter Sunday is by far the most important day in the Church calendar. It represents new birth and hope for the world, as it is the day of Christ's resurrection and the day of new and eternal life, a time for much joy and celebration.

We associate eggs, especially chocolate ones, with this day, but rich creamy desserts, spring lamb and Easter rabbits, along with other symbols of new life, have come to represent this special day. Eggs are also a pagan reminder that spring is a time of hopeful fertility for good crops and produce for the months ahead.

The lamb slaughtered as part of the traditional Jewish Passover has been adopted by the Christian Church as a symbol of the sacrifice of Christ. New season's roast lamb has become the traditional meal for Easter Sunday. Young lamb, a delicate pink colour with a subtle flavour, is also a reminder that spring is here. It is usually enjoyed with fresh spring herbs, particularly mint made into a sauce with vinegar. We celebrate the day with a Sunday brunch and/or lunch.

EASTER SUNDAY BRUNCH

Sultana and Chocolate Bread
Chocolate and Hazelnut Ganache
Mushroom, Sage and Goat's Cheese Soufflé Omelette
Parma Eggs Benedict
Coddled Eggs with Kippers

Serve these light dishes with a sparkling Petaluma from Australia.

EASTER SUNDAY LUNCH

SERVES 6

Spring Vegetable and Mint Pesto Soup
Pot-roast Lamb with Spring Onions and Jersey Royals
Steamed Banana and Chocolate Chip Pudding

Serve the soup with toasted or cold Italian bread, such as ciabatta or foccaccia, and the roast lamb with baby spring vegetables. This lunch would be well matched with any Gran Reserva Rioja.

Sultana and Chocolate Bread

450g (1lb/3½ cups) strong plain flour

1 tsp salt

1 tbsp fresh or 2 tsp dried yeast

55g (2oz/scant ½ cup) caster sugar

200ml (7fl oz/⁷/8 cup) milk

1 egg, beaten

85g (3oz/³/8 cup) butter, softened

1 tsp mixed spice

55g (2oz/⅓ cup) sultanas

55g (2oz/⅓ cup) dark chocolate, chopped

55g (2oz/⅓ cup) milk chocolate, chopped

Icing sugar, to serve

Sift the flour and salt together into a large bowl. Mix the yeast with 1 tsp of the sugar until it forms a liquid. Make a well in the centre of the flour and add the yeast mix, milk and egg. Stir until the mixture comes together to make a soft, but not sticky, dough. Turn the dough on to a lightly floured board and knead for 8–10min, or until smooth.

Place the dough in a lightly oiled bowl, cover with cling film and leave to rise in a warm place for 1 hour, or until it has doubled in size.

Once it has risen, turn the dough on to a floured board and knead it again for 2–3min. Roll the dough into a 40x30cm (16x12in) rectangle.

Spread the butter over the dough, then sprinkle on the remaining sugar, mixed spice, sultanas and chocolate, and run a rolling pin over the top to press them gently into the dough. Roll the dough lengthwise into a sausage and place it, seam side down, on a greased tray. Cover with greaseproof paper and leave to prove (rise a second time) for 15min.

Heat the oven to 200ºC (400ºF/gas mark 6).

Bake the bread on the top shelf of the oven for 10min, then reduce the temperature to 180ºC (350ºF/gas mark 4) and bake for a further 30min, or until well risen and cooked – it will sound hollow when tapped on the underside.

Transfer the bread to a wire rack and leave to cool for 10min. Dust very heavily with icing sugar, and serve.

Chocolate and Hazelnut Ganache

This rich chocolate ganache is a wonderful, if rich, spread for bread. It can also be used for icing a cake.

225g (8oz/1 cup) plain chocolate, chopped into small pieces

110g (4oz/1/2 cup) milk chocolate, chopped into small pieces

85g (3oz/3/8 cup) unsalted butter

150ml (1/4 pint/5/8 cup) double cream

110g (4oz/1 cup) toasted hazelnuts, chopped

Place the chocolate in a heatproof glass bowl with the butter, and set it over a saucepan of simmering water (don't allow the water to touch the bowl). Stir continuously until the chocolate has melted.

Add the double cream, mix in well and allow the chocolate to cool slightly. Add the hazelnuts, then cover the bowl and chill, to allow the mixture to set to a smooth paste.

To serve, spread the ganache on toasted bread, brioche or Sultana and Chocolate Bread.

Mushroom, Sage and Goat's Cheese Soufflé Omelette

SERVES 2

45g (1 1/2oz/1/6 cup) butter

170g (6oz/1 1/2 cups) cup mushrooms, thinly sliced

1 tbsp chopped sage

85g (3oz/1/2 cup) goat's cheese, coarsely grated

4 eggs, separated

Melt 30g (1oz) of the butter in a frying pan until hot and foaming. Add the mushrooms and sauté over a high heat for 3–4min, or until cooked. Add the sage and season with salt and pepper. Transfer to a bowl and add the cheese.

Place the egg yolks in a small bowl and season with salt and pepper. In a separate clean, dry bowl, whisk the egg whites until they form medium stiff peaks and fold the two egg mixes together.

Melt the remaining butter in a frying pan until it foams. Pour the egg mixture in and cook over a very low heat for 4–5min, or until just set.

Add the mushroom mixture to one side of the omelette, fold it in half and transfer to a plate. Serve very hot.

Parma Eggs Benedict

SERVES 4

For the mock hollandaise sauce:

2 egg yolks

3 tbsp Greek yoghurt

A splash of lemon juice

2 tbsp freshly grated Parmesan cheese

A pinch of cayenne pepper

4 eggs

2 English muffins

15g (¹/₂oz/¹/₂ tbsp) butter

4 slices Parma ham, fat removed

1 tbsp chopped chives

Heat the grill to its highest setting.

Mix the sauce ingredients together and season with salt and pepper.

Poach the eggs in a poaching pan until the egg white is set, but the yolk is still runny.

Split the muffins in half and toast the cut side for 2min under the grill. Spread with a little butter. Arrange the Parma ham on top, add an egg and spoon the mock hollandaise sauce mixture over.

Grill for a further 1–2min or until the top is lightly browned, then sprinkle with the chives and serve immediately.

Coddled Eggs with Kippers

SERVES 4

1 kipper

150ml (¹/₄ pint/⁵/₈ cup) milk

4 eggs

4 tbsp single cream

A pinch of grated nutmeg

2 tbsp grated Gruyère cheese

Heat the oven to 180ºC (350ºF/gas mark 4).

Place the kipper in a saucepan with the milk, bring to the boil, cover and remove from the heat. Leave to stand for 10min. Remove the kipper, pulling away the skin, and break it into flakes, taking out any bones in the process.

Divide the fish between four ramekins. Break an egg on the top of each. Mix the cream, nutmeg and cheese together, season to taste with salt and pepper and spoon over the eggs.

Set the ramekins in a roasting tin half-filled with boiling water.

Bake for 12–15min, or until the egg whites are set, but the yolk is still runny. Serve immediately.

Spring Vegetable and Mint Pesto Soup

SERVES 6

225g (8oz) baby turnips

225g (8oz) baby carrots

340g (12oz) new potatoes

30g (1oz/¹/₈ cup) butter

1 onion, finely chopped

1ltr (1³/₄ pints/4¹/₂ cups) well-flavoured vegetable stock

For the pesto:

A large handful of mint leaves

2 tbsp toasted almonds

1 clove garlic, crushed

3 tbsp virgin olive oil

4 tbsp freshly grated Parmesan cheese

Trim the turnips, carrots and potatoes, and cut into chunks.

Heat the butter in a frying pan and cook the onion for 7–10min, or until soft. Add the vegetables and toss over a low heat for a further 5min. Pour on the vegetable stock, bring to the boil and simmer for 10–12min, or until the vegetables are tender.

Transfer the vegetables and stock to a liquidizer and whizz to form a smooth purée. Return the purée to the rinsed-out saucepan. Season with salt and pepper to taste and set aside.

Put the ingredients for the pesto into the rinsed-out liquidizer, and whizz to form a paste. Season to taste with salt and pepper and set aside.

To serve, warm the soup and add the mint pesto, then heat to scalding point, but don't allow it to boil.

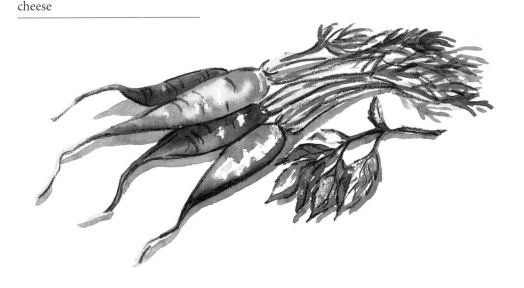

Pot-roast Lamb with Spring Onions and Jersey Royals

SERVES 6

1.35kg (3lb) shoulder of lamb

30g (1oz/$^1/8$ cup) butter

6 cloves garlic, unpeeled

2 sprigs of rosemary

2 sprigs of thyme

2 bay leaves

150ml ($^1/4$ pint/$^5/8$ cup) dry red wine

150ml ($^1/4$ pint/$^5/8$ cup) vegetable stock

1 tbsp redcurrant jelly

900g (2lb) Jersey Royals or other new potatoes, scrubbed

12 spring onions, cut into 5cm (2in) lengths

1$^1/2$ tbsp mint sauce

Arrowroot, as required

Heat the oven to 180°C (350°F/gas mark 4).

Trim the lamb, removing any excess fat. Score the fat across the top of the joint and spread half of the butter over it. Season well with salt and freshly ground black pepper.

Melt the remaining butter in a large casserole pot. Brown the lamb quickly on each side, then add the garlic, herbs, wine, stock and redcurrant jelly. Bring to the boil and cover with a tight-fitting lid.

Cook in the oven for 30min, then remove, arrange the potatoes around the edge of the lamb, re-cover and continue to pot-roast, adding the spring onions after 30min, until the lamb is cooked, which will take 1–1$^1/4$ hours. If you like the lamb pink, reduce the cooking time a little.

Remove the lamb from the pot and place on a serving dish, arranging the potatoes and spring onions around the edge. Set aside while you make the gravy.

Strain the cooking juices into a jug, pressing well to extract as much flavour as possible from the herbs and garlic, and skim away the excess fat. Pour the remaining liquid into a saucepan and bring to the boil. Add the mint sauce and season with salt and pepper. Mix 1 tsp arrowroot with a little cold water and blend it into the simmering gravy, then bring the gravy back to the boil, adding more arrowroot if it's too thin. Pour into a jug and serve.

Steamed Banana and Chocolate Chip Pudding

SERVES 6

110g (4oz/^{1}/$_2$ cup) block margarine

110g (4oz/^{5}/$_8$ cup) dark brown sugar

3 eggs

2 ripe bananas, peeled and mashed

85g (3oz/^{3}/$_4$ cup) milk chocolate, chopped

225g (8oz/1^1/$_4$ cups) self-raising flour

2 tbsp milk

Single cream, to serve

Cream the margarine and sugar together until light and fluffy. Beat the eggs and add to the pudding mixture, a little at a time, then stir in the bananas and chocolate.

Sift the flour and fold into the mixture with the milk until the pudding has a soft dropping consistency.

Spoon the mixture into a buttered 1.35ltr (2 pint) pudding basin. Cover it with greaseproof paper and aluminium foil, tied securely with string. Put the basin into a large saucepan and pour boiling water into it, to come ^{2}/$_3$ of the way up the sides of the basin. Cover the saucepan with a tight-fitting lid and steam for 1^1/$_2$ hours. Check the level of the water every so often and add more boiling water if necessary – don't allow the saucepan to boil dry.

The pudding is cooked when it feels spongy to the touch. Unwrap and check it after 1^1/$_2$ hours, then rewrap and continue to steam if necessary. When cooked, loosen the pudding from the basin with a round bladed knife and turn it on to a warm plate. Serve with single cream.

ST DAVID'S FEAST DAY

St David, patron saint of Wales, is commemorated on 1 March. David was a monk and bishop of the sixth century; little is known about his life, but he became the patron saint of Wales as early as the twelfth century.

There are many ingredients and recipes that are particularly associated with Wales: saltmarsh lamb, fabulous seafood, particularly crab, cockles and sewin (seatrout), laverbread (seaweed), many different types of cheese and, last but not at all least, the national symbol – leeks. Our menu celebrates some of these good ingredients from Wales.

ST DAVID'S DAY SUPPER

SERVES 4

Crab and Cockle Chowder
Glazed Lamb Chumps with Sautéed Leeks

Serve the chowder with crusty bread or Oat and Sunflower Bread Rolls (see page 98). To complete the meal, choose a bright, crisp bitter leaf salad to add texture and colour. Instead of a sweet dessert, finish the meal with seasonal fruit and a good wedge of Caerphilly cheese.

A Cru Beaujolais, such as Julienas, will cope well with these strong flavours.

Crab and Cockle Chowder

This soup is substantial, so serve a moderate amount as a first course.

SERVES 4

55g (2oz/¼ cup) unsalted butter

1 small onion, finely sliced

2 sticks celery, sliced

1 parsnip or turnip, peeled and diced

1 orange-fleshed sweet potato, peeled and diced

1 gammon steak, de-rinded and diced

2 tbsp flour

600ml (1 pint/2½ cups) hot milk

110g (4oz/½ cup) white crab meat

½ tsp nutmeg

A pinch of cayenne pepper

110g (4oz/½ cup) cockles in brine, drained

1 tbsp chopped chives or Welsh onion tops

sMelt half of the butter in a large saucepan, add the vegetables and diced gammon and stir over a moderate heat for 5–7 min, or until the vegetables are lightly browned.

Add the flour and stir for 1min, then pour the hot milk on gradually, stirring all the while to form a sauce. Bring to the boil and simmer for 5min, or until the vegetables are tender, but not breaking up. Season to taste with salt and pepper.

Mix the crab meat with the remaining butter, nutmeg and cayenne pepper.

Stir into the hot chowder and add the cockles. Heat through for a few minutes until the chowder is piping hot, but don't allow the soup to come to a rapid boil. Sprinkle with chives and serve.

Glazed Lamb Chumps
with Sautéed Leeks

Laverbread, a seaweed that grows along the Welsh coastline, is a traditional accompaniment to the lamb that wanders among the hills. It's not easy to come across, but if you do, stir some into the creamed leeks just before serving.

SERVES 4

4x170g (6oz) lamb chump chops

2 tbsp redcurrant jelly

1 tbsp mint sauce

55g (2oz/¼ cup) butter

8 leeks, finely sliced

1 clove garlic, crushed

4 tbsp double cream (optional)

Freshly grated nutmeg

Laverbread (if available), chopped, to serve

Sprigs of mint, to garnish

Trim the excess fat off the lamb chumps, brush them with the redcurrant jelly and mint sauce and season well with salt and pepper. Set aside.

Melt the butter in a large saucepan, add the leeks and garlic, cover with a piece of dampened greaseproof paper and cook over a very low heat for 12–15min, or until the leeks are soft – they burn easily, so stir them frequently.

When the leeks are soft, add the double cream (if using) and nutmeg, and season to taste with salt and pepper. Set aside.

Heat the grill to its highest setting. Cook the lamb chumps for 4–6min on each side – the time will vary enormously, depending on the thickness of the meat and the colour required.

Stir in the laverbread, if using, then divide the creamed leeks between four dinner plates and arrange a piece of lamb on top. Garnish with mint, and serve.

ST PATRICK'S FEAST DAY

The patron saint of Ireland, Patrick was born in Britain in the fifth century and, according to legend, attributed with driving all the snakes from Ireland. He came to believe in God and became one of the early Celtic preachers. He eventually moved to Ireland, where he established a church and encouraged men and women to become monks and nuns. His feast day is celebrated on 17 March: it is a national holiday in Ireland.

Our menu for St Patrick's Day is a family supper featuring some of the wonderful produce that Ireland is particularly famous for, which includes the dark stout of the River Liffey – Guinness.

The Irish have a well-deserved reputation for their baked goods: a meal would not be complete without soda bread. Other well-loved recipes include that for barm brack, a yeasted fruit bread which is particularly popular at New Year, St Brigid's Day on 1 February and Halloween. Potatoes feature frequently in many traditional recipes: boxty, potato griddlecakes usually eaten on All Saints' Day; fadge, a potato bread; and colcannon, the famous mashed potato dish.

ST PATRICK'S DAY SUPPER

SERVES 6

Beef, Guinness and Smoked Oyster Casserole
Colcannon
Grilled Cashel Blue with Spiced Pear Jam
Malted Soda Bread

Serve a St Emilion from Chateau BelAir with this meal.

Beef, Guinness and Smoked Oyster Casserole

SERVES 6

30g (1oz/⅛ cup) butter

1 large onion, finely sliced

2 cloves garlic, crushed

2 sticks celery

1 carrot, peeled and thickly sliced

2 tbsp flour

300ml (½ pint/1¼ cups) well-flavoured brown stock

1.5kg (3¼ lb) stewing steak

2 tbsp sunflower oil

600ml (1 pint/2½ cups) Guinness

1 bay leaf

Sprig of thyme

1 tsp grated nutmeg

1 tbsp dark brown sugar

1 tbsp malt vinegar

225g (8oz) smoked oysters

1 tbsp chopped parsley

Heat the oven to 150ºC (300ºF/gas mark 2).

Heat the butter in a large casserole pot and cook the onion for 20–25min or until golden brown. Add the garlic, celery, carrot and flour, and stir over a low heat for 2–3min. Add half of the stock, bring to the boil and pour into a bowl.

Add the sunflower oil to the pot, and brown the stewing steak very well, a few pieces at a time, keeping the browned meat aside. Add the Guinness to the pot, bring to the boil and simmer for 3–4min.

Return the meat, onion mixture and stock to the pot, bring to the boil and add the herbs, nutmeg, sugar and vinegar. Season lightly with salt and pepper.

Cover the pot with a tight-fitting lid and cook in the oven for 1½–2 hours, or until the beef is tender.

Remove the beef from the pot and set aside. Bring the liquid to the boil and skim away any fat, if necessary, then add the smoked oysters, adjust the seasoning and cook for a further 3–4min on a low heat.

Return the meat to the pot, add the parsley, and serve.

Colcannon

SERVES 6

675g (1½ lb) potatoes, peeled and cut into chunks

225g (8oz) spring greens

150ml (¼ pint/⅝ cup) single cream

55g (2oz/¼ cup) butter

Cook the potatoes in boiling, salted water until tender, then drain and push through a sieve.

Cook the spring greens in boiling, salted water until tender, then refresh under running cold water and drain. Shred very finely.

Mix the potatoes and spring greens together, stir in the cream and season well with salt and pepper.

Heat the butter in a large frying pan and add the potato mixture. Lower the heat and cook gently for 2–3min, then break up the colcannon with a fork and continue to fry for a further few minutes, or until very hot. Serve immediately.

Grilled Cashel Blue with Spiced Pear Jam

Cashel Blue is an award-winning cheese from Tipperary.

SERVES 6

30g (1oz/⅛ cup) butter

85g (3oz/½ cup) soft brown sugar

4 pears, peeled, cored and diced

1 tsp ground cinnamon

1 tsp mixed spice

2 tbsp raisins

2 tbsp cider vinegar

2–3 tbsp Irish whiskey or apple juice

340g (12oz) piece Cashel Blue cheese

6 slices Malted Soda Bread (see page 132)

To make the jam, melt the butter in a saucepan, and add the sugar, pears, spices, raisins, cider vinegar and whiskey. Cover with damp greaseproof paper and cook over a very low heat for 15–20min, or until the pears are soft and beginning to break up. Transfer the mix to a bowl and leave to cool.

Heat a grill to its highest setting.

Remove any rind from the cheese and dice finely. Toast the slices of bread for a few seconds on each side. Divide the cheese between the slices of bread and grill until the cheese is beginning to soften, but not melt. Serve immediately with a spoonful of pear jam on the side.

Malted Soda Bread

340g (12oz/2¼ cups) plain flour

1 tsp salt

1 rounded tsp bicarbonate of soda

2 tbsp malt extract

250–300ml (8–10fl oz/1–1¼ cups) buttermilk

Heat the oven to 190°C (375°F/gas mark 5). Lightly dust a baking sheet with flour.

Sift the flour, salt and bicarbonate of soda into a large bowl. Mix the malt extract and buttermilk together and add to the flour, a little at a time, until a soft, but not sticky, dough is formed.

Place the dough on the baking sheet and shape it into a round, leaving the surface and shape quite rough. Mark a cross on the top and dust with a little flour. Bake in the centre of the oven for 25min.

Reduce the oven temperature to 180°C (350°F/gas mark 4) and bake for a further 15–20min, or until the base of the bread sounds hollow when tapped and a dark crust has formed. Transfer bread to a wire rack to cool.

ST GEORGE'S FEAST DAY

The patron saint of England, the feast of St George is celebrated on 23 April. He is also the patron saint of soldiers and it is thought that George was a soldier himself in the fourth century. The legend tells that George saved a country from a dragon by first capturing and finally slaying the beast, and continues that in return for slaying the dragon, the King and his people were baptized in the aftermath of this heroic deed. George was subsequently persecuted and martyred for his faith.

To celebrate St George's Day, here is a dinner menu influenced by traditional ingredients and recipes from England.

ST GEORGE'S DAY DINNER

SERVES 6

English Cheese and Apple Savoury
Pan-roast Sirloin Steaks with a Pepper and Mustard Seed Crust
Bacon Yorkshire Puddings
Onion and Thyme Gravy
Horseradish and King Edward Mash
Lemon, Lime and White Chocolate Syllabub

To complete the menu, serve the beef and Yorkshire puddings with spring greens. Cheese and apples are traditionally eaten together at the end of a meal in many parts of Britain, but they are combined instead in a hot first course in this menu; a savoury such as this can equally be eaten at the beginning or end of a meal. A superb Chianti Classico from Isole e Olena, Tuscany, is an ideal wine for this meal.

English Cheese and Apple Savoury

MAKES 12 FINGERS

3 slices of wholemeal bread

55g (2oz/^{1}/4 cup) mature Cheddar cheese, grated

55g (2oz/^{1}/4 cup) Stilton cheese, crumbled

55g (2oz/^{1}/4 cup) Cheshire cheese, grated

4 tbsp cider

^{1}/2 tsp dried English mustard

1 egg yolk

A pinch of cayenne pepper

30g (1oz/^{1}/8 cup) butter

3 tbsp soft dark brown sugar

1 tsp ground cinnamon

1 dessert apple, cored and diced

Heat the grill to its highest setting and lightly toast the bread on both sides.

Mix together the cheeses, cider, mustard, egg yolk and cayenne pepper, season with ground black pepper and set aside.

Melt the butter in a large frying pan and add the sugar, cinnamon and apple. Fry over a very high heat for 4–5min, or until the apples are golden brown.

Spoon a little apple mixture over the toasted bread, top with some cheese mixture and grill on a low shelf for 2–3min, or until the cheese has a golden crust.

Remove the crusts from the bread and divide each slice into three. Serve very hot.

Pan-roast Sirloin Steaks with a Pepper and Mustard Seed Crust

SERVES 6

6 x 225g (8oz) sirloin or fillet
steaks at least 2.5cm (1in) thick

For the crust:

3tbsp Worcestershire sauce

2tbsp coarsely ground mixed
peppercorns (black, white
and pink)

1tbsp green peppercorns, drained
and finely chopped

2tbsp yellow mustard seeds

1tbsp coarse-grain mustard

4tbsp fresh white breadcrumbs

1tbsp finely chopped parsley

1tbsp chopped chives

30g (1oz/⅛ cup) butter, melted

A little oil or melted dripping

Heat the oven to 220°C (425°F/gas mark 7). Remove
the steaks from the refrigerator 30min before you want
to cook them.

Mix together all the ingredients for the crust
and season to taste with salt.

Brush each steak with the oil or melted dripping.
Heat a large frying pan until it starts to smoke and sear
each steak very quickly on both sides. Transfer to a
roasting tin.

Divide the crust mixture between the steaks and press
it on to the upper side of each piece of meat. Cook in
the oven for 7–10min or to taste, remove from the
roasting tin and serve.

Onion and Thyme Gravy

Makes 600ml (1 pint); serves 6

3 tbsp dripping or grapeseed oil

3 large onions, peeled and very finely sliced

1 tbsp malt vinegar

1 tbsp soft dark brown sugar

1 tbsp flour

600ml (1 pint/2½ cups) well-seasoned brown stock

1 tbsp chopped thyme

Heat the dripping or oil in a saucepan and cook the onions over a very low heat for 1 hour, until rich golden brown. To prevent the onions from burning, cover with a piece of dampened greaseproof paper and a lid, and stir every so often – if they still burn, add a splash of cold water.

Add the malt vinegar, sugar and flour to the pan and stir over a low heat for a further 3–4min. Add the stock and season to taste with salt and pepper.

Bring to the boil and simmer for 15min, or until the gravy becomes syrupy. Stir in the thyme and serve.

Bacon Yorkshire Puddings

Makes 12

2 rashers streaky bacon, rind removed, finely chopped

110g (4oz/⅔ cup) plain flour

1 egg

1 egg yolk

150ml (¼ pint/⅝ cup) cold water

150ml (¼ pint/⅝ cup) milk

1 tbsp dripping or sunflower oil

Heat the oven to 220°C (425°F/gas mark 7).

Fry the bacon in a small frying pan until brown and crisp, then set aside, taking care to reserve any bacon fat that has been rendered during cooking.

Sift the flour into a small basin, make a well in the centre and add the whole egg, the egg yolk and half of the measured water. Stir the liquid, gradually incorporating the flour, until a smooth batter is formed and, as it thickens, add the remaining water and the milk. Season lightly with pepper, add the bacon and stir.

Mix any remaining bacon fat with the dripping or oil. Use this fat to grease a 12-mould bun tin generously. Heat the tin in the oven for 2–3min, then pour the batter into the moulds until they're two-thirds full.

Bake for 15–18min, or until well risen and golden brown. Serve immediately.

Horseradish and King Edward Mash

SERVES 6

1.35kg (3lb) King Edward potatoes, peeled and cut into large chunks

150–200ml (¹/₄–¹/₃ pint/⁵/₈–⁷/₈ cup) buttermilk

55g (2oz/¹/₄ cup) butter

4 tbsp creamed or 2 tbsp fresh grated horseradish

1 tsp grated nutmeg

Cook the potatoes in plenty of boiling, salted water until tender. Drain and push through a sieve.

Return the potatoes to the pan, push them to one side and add two-thirds of the buttermilk, the butter and the creamed horseradish to the other side of the pan. Heat to scalding point and stir into the potatoes.

Season with the nutmeg and salt and pepper and set aside. If you need to keep the potatoes warm, leave them in the saucepan and pour over the remaining buttermilk – when you're ready to serve, beat the buttermilk into the potatoes over a very low heat to warm through.

Lemon, Lime
and White Chocolate Syllabub

Syllabub is thought to be an Elizabethan dish, made from milk, cream and mead. The recipes with which we are familiar today are usually a rich concoction of whipped cream and alcohol.

SERVES 6

Pared zest of a lemon and a lime, cut into very thin shreds

55g (2oz/¼ cup) granulated sugar

---

5 tbsp water

300ml (½ pint/1¼ cups) double cream

300ml (½ pint/1¼ cups) Greek yoghurt

Juice of 1 lemon

Juice of 2 limes

125ml (4fl oz/½ cup) Sauternes or other sweet dessert wine

110g (4oz/½ cup) white chocolate, grated

Place the citrus zest in a small saucepan and cover with water. Bring to the boil, simmer for 5min, then drain.

Place the sugar and water in the saucepan and stir over a low heat until the sugar dissolves. Add the citrus zest and cook over a medium heat until the water has evaporated and the zest is sticky. Transfer the zest to a plate and leave to cool.

Whip the cream until stiff and fold in the yoghurt, citrus juice and Sauternes. Add the white chocolate and most of the cooked zest.

Spoon the syllabub into six large wine glasses, cover and chill until required.

To serve, sprinkle the reserved citrus zest over the top.

Summer Feasts

With the cycle of Easter nearing completion, the Church moves into a quiet period, although many well-known feasts and saints' days take place during the warm summer months. Summer, however, is a busy time for the earth and for family life. For many it is a holiday period.

Two commercial holidays present themselves during May, the first celebrating spring and Labour Day, the second at the end of May, usually around the time of Ascension or Whitsunday. They are both an opportunity for a family gathering; the weather is becoming warmer and people are beginning to think about the garden and their plans for the summer.

Ascension and the Whitsunday weekend are both moveable feasts. Ascension Day is celebrated forty days after Easter. One of the greatest feasts celebrated within the Church, it commemorates the ascension of the risen Jesus to heaven. The day always falls on a Thursday, and is usually celebrated with a service or early morning mass.

Whitsunday celebrates the anointing of the apostles by the Holy Spirit; this is the beginning of their ministry, spreading the message that Jesus Christ brought to the world. The Whitsun weekend is spread over three days. Things quieten down after Whitsunday and the Church moves into 'ordinary' time. In days gone by, long hours of outdoor agricultural work probably took precedence as those working the land made the most of the long days of summer daylight.

Summer is an ideal time for family celebrations. Christenings and dedications traditionally took place at Whitsun, and they provide the perfect occasion for a family gathering. Wedding feasts, too, are a pivotal part of family life and although they are held at most times during the course of the year, June is the traditional month for wedding celebrations. Christ performed his first miracle at a wedding when he turned water into wine.

Birthdays are both a personal and family celebration. It is customary in the Catholic Church to name one's child after a saint, and traditionally it was important to celebrate the feast of one's saint in preference to one's actual birth date. Saints' days have always played a role in everyday life. Not only countries, but also those suffering various ailments or employed in various occupations have their own patron saint. For a cook it is Martha, for a grocer St Michael, and the patron saint of pastry cooks is St Honore. Even broadcasters are fittingly under the patronage of Gabriel, who according to Scripture delivered so many important messages from God.

The summer solstice was celebrated by the Celts in the middle of June. The longest day as it stands now is on 21 June, although midsummer celebrations begin on St John's Day, 24 June. The month of June was usually busy with haymaking and other harvesting activities, but time would be made for the traditional pagan rituals of bonfires and fortune-telling. St Barnabas and the fisherman, St Peter, also celebrate their feast days on 11 and 29 June respectively. The commercial celebration of Father's Day is a modern invention which also usually takes place in June.

As summer progresses, the American Day of Independence is celebrated with fireworks and a national holiday on 4 July. The feast of St Swithin, a bishop of Winchester in the ninth century, is celebrated on 15 July. If it rains on this day, legend says that it will rain for a further forty days. One of the patron saints of fishermen (there are several), St James is celebrated on 23 July, and St Martha on 29 July.

The holiday time of August was in past times the month for fairs; many people, especially those in service, took leave from their place of employment for an annual holiday at this time. August was also the month when many towns would celebrate their saint's day feasts. These days became known as wakes in some parts of the UK. The saint's day would begin with a dawn service celebration. Lammas Day on 1 August would get the ball rolling. The day celebrated the Celtic quarter year-end and was another festival of fertility. It was traditionally the day that the first bread was made with the new year's corn.

The game season opens on 12 August, a day better known as the Glorious Twelfth. This is the first day of the grouse season, celebrated on the moors in Northern England and Scotland.

Harvest festival is celebrated at different times in various parts of the world. In the northern hemisphere we celebrate the abundance of summer fruits during June, July and August by making jams and jellies. The autumn harvest is also celebrated with the making of chutneys and pickles come late August and September. The feast of St Bartholomew, the patron saint of beekeepers, is on 24 August – it is the customary day for harvesting the summer honey.

SEASONAL INGREDIENTS IN SUMMER

We are fortunate these days to have most fruit and vegetables available at any time of the year. But how many times have you felt disappointed with a strawberry or tomato in the middle of winter? There is a season for everything, and more often than not a fruit or vegetable that has had the benefit of good sunlight and a good growing season will taste the best.

The warmth of summer is a wonderful time for homegrown produce. By the end of May seasonal produce is really coming into its own and choice is exceptional, with a huge variety available on our doorstep. Summertime cooking is always varied and easy.

Early summer brings the first English cherries, but also the start of the soft berry season: strawberries, raspberries and currants. Gooseberries are ripening on the bush now and will have lost their sharp acidity – they will have turned to a soft golden pink and can be eaten raw. Don't forget the classic match of elderflowers and gooseberries – their seasons coincide.

Top fruits such as greengages, peaches, apricots and nectarines are available virtually all year round, but in August many are imported from warmer parts of Europe and have had the benefit of the summer sun, so they are really worth looking out for.

By Whitsunday the first green peas should be ready for picking, as are broad beans, which have a wonderful flavour and pop easily from the pod. By the time July comes, many varieties of beans – runners, French, dwarf, sugar snaps, mange tout and string – will be in plentiful supply.

Shoots and stalks are all flourishing. Rhubarb is more mature: its season continues right through the summer. English asparagus is around during May and June, so its price is still good. Artichokes, seakale and Florence fennel are also in plentiful supply by June.

We are inundated with as extensive selection of salad leaves at this time of the year. All the supermarkets prepare bags of many different kinds of mixed leaves all through the year, but buying home-produced individual lettuces at this time of year makes lots of sense. Wash and spin lettuce dry and it will keep crisp in a salad drawer for a few days.

Early new potatoes (usually in season from May to July) are all in full swing by now and there are plenty of varieties to choose from. The early varieties of potatoes are lifted when the plants are still immature and the skins are still not 'set', so they can be scrubbed clean. These new potatoes do not tend to store well. Second early potatoes are harvested in late summer; they have a thicker skin and will store well through the winter, making new potatoes available through most of the year.

English hothouse vegetables, including aubergines, peppers, chillies and tomatoes, are ripening and are ready for eating by August. Courgettes are available in mid-July and marrows by late August or September. They should be of excellent quality and the price low.

If we have had a really good hot summer, chances are that homegrown sweetcorn will be particularly good – sweet, tender and, importantly, inexpensive too. It starts to make an appearance in August.

Many young root vegetables such as turnips, beetroot, carrots and radishes are also wonderful at this time. Some say that small vegetables lack depth of flavour but blanched, glazed baby turnips and carrots are a lovely vegetable accompaniment; they are still very sweet and full of flavour.

The coarse-leaved herbs such as parsley (under cloches), rosemary, thyme, bay and sage are always plentiful during the year. The soft delicate herbs, chives, basil, tarragon, chervil and oregano, are annuals and grow and die each summer. They are available at a price from most supermarkets all year round, but growing some in the garden or window box is easy and fulfilling.

Summer Berry Kissel Sponge Cake

225g (8oz/1 cup) block margarine

225g (8oz/1 cup) caster sugar

4 medium eggs, beaten

225g (8oz/1¾ cups) self-raising flour, sifted with ½ tsp baking powder

1 tsp vanilla essence

1–2 tbsp cold milk

For the filling:

225g (8oz/1 cup) mixed blackcurrants and redcurrants

170g (6oz/¾ cup) raspberries

170g (6oz/¾ cup) strawberries

Grated zest and juice of ½ orange

110g (4oz/1 cup) icing sugar

1–2 tbsp cornflour

3 tbsp water

225ml (8fl oz/1 cup) double cream, lightly whipped

Icing sugar, to dust

30g (1oz/¼ cup) each white and dark chocolate, melted, to decorate

Heat the oven to 180°C (350°F/gas mark 4). Lightly oil a 25cm (10in) spring-form tin and line the base with non-stick baking parchment.

Cream the margarine and sugar together until very pale and fluffy. Add the eggs, a splash at a time, until they are all incorporated. If you add the eggs too quickly, the mixture will curdle; if this happens, stir in 1 tbsp of the flour and continue adding the eggs.

Sift the flour and baking powder on to the cake mixture and add the vanilla essence. Fold the mixture together, adding enough milk to bring the mixture to a soft dropping consistency. Spoon it into the prepared tin and make a slight indentation in the centre to ensure the cake rises evenly.

Bake in the centre of the oven for 30–35min or until the cake springs back to the touch and is beginning to shrink away from the edge of the tin. Remove from the oven and leave to cool for 3–4min.

Loosen the cake and release the spring-form tin. Transfer to a wire rack and leave to cool for 30min.

Meanwhile, make the fruit filling. Take 110g (4oz/½ cup) of the mixed currants and remove the stalks using the prongs of a fork. Rinse well and place in a saucepan with 55g (2oz/¼ cup) each of raspberries and strawberries, the orange zest and juice and the icing sugar. Stir well, bring to the boil over a low flame and simmer, still stirring, for 7–10min, or until the fruit is just beginning to soften. Mix the cornflour with the water and stir into the fruit. Bring back to the boil, then transfer to a bowl to cool.

To assemble the cake, split the sponge in half using a bread knife. Spread a thin layer of the cream on the lower half, then the cold fruit kissel over the top. Reassemble the cake. Spread the remaining cream on top of the cake and arrange the fresh fruit in a generous pile on top. Dust with icing sugar.

Fill two greaseproof piping bags with the melted chocolate, one dark and one white, and drizzle over the fruit in a zig-zag pattern. Leave to set for 10min before serving.

WHITSUN

In the second half of May or sometimes at the beginning of June, we celebrate the feast of Whitsun. It is also an important day for the Church: it is the time of Pentecost, which during the life and times of Jesus was a celebrated Jewish festival of thanksgiving. Ten days after the ascension of Jesus, the Holy Spirit visited the apostles to anoint them in preparation for continuing the work that Jesus had begun. Whitsun or 'white Sunday' is represented by white doves, a symbol of the Holy Spirit and of Pentecost. It is a traditional time for baptisms and dedications and a time for beginning a new journey.

The traditional meal for Whitsun in England is a young roast duckling, served with the first pickings of the new season's peas. Depending on the weather the wild elderflower is blooming. Gooseberries are usually in season about the same time and the two are paired together in many classic combinations – gooseberries are a traditional fruit to serve at Whitsun.

We celebrate this holiday time with a family lunch for six, which uses these and many of the other ingredients that are coming into season by late May or the beginning of June.

WHITSUN LUNCH

SERVES 6

Roast Duck Breasts with Herb Crackling
Baked New Potatoes
Minted Sugar Snaps, Baby Gem Lettuce and Asparagus
Gooseberry Crumble with Elderflower Custard
or Kentish Cherry Compôte with Treacle Snaps

Serve a good Californian Merlot with this lunch.

Roast Duck Breasts with Herb Crackling

The duck requires marinating for 1–2 hours before cooking.

SERVES 6

6 duck breasts

Oil and salt, for crackling

1 tbsp chopped sage

1 tbsp chopped mint

6 tbsp wholemeal breadcrumbs

4 spring onions, finely chopped

2 tbsp ginger wine

Grated zest of 1 orange

Apple and Bay Jelly (see page 205), to serve

Heat the oven to 220°C (425°F/gas mark 7).

Remove the skin from the duck, rub the skin with a little salt and oil and place it on a baking sheet. Roast for 15min, or until very crisp, then drain off the fat and set aside. Chop the crackling roughly. Mix the crackling with the herbs, breadcrumbs and spring onions, and season to taste with salt and pepper. Set aside.

Make two or three slashes into the duck breast, season it with pepper and place it on a shallow tray. Dribble the ginger wine and sprinkle the orange zest over the top, and leave to marinate for 1–2 hours.

Heat a little of the reserved duck oil in a large griddle pan, season the duck breasts with a little salt and pan-fry for 1min on each side. Place the pan-fried meat on a roasting tin and roast for 6–7min, or just cooked to taste.

In the meantime, heat the remaining duck fat in the griddle pan, add the herb crackling and toss over a high heat until toasted.

Sprinkle the crackling over the duck, and serve.

Baked New Potatoes

SERVES 6

675g (1¹/₂ lb) small new potatoes

1 tbsp sunflower oil

1 tsp ground nutmeg

Coarse ground rock salt

2 bay leaves

Heat the oven to 200°C (400°F/gas mark 6).

Scrub the potatoes to remove the loose skin and pat dry with absorbent paper.

Mix the sunflower oil, nutmeg and a generous shaking of rock salt, and season with black pepper. Add the bay leaves and new potatoes and toss to coat lightly.

Spread the potatoes in a single layer in a roasting tin and bake for 30–40min, or until tender. Drain any excess oil from the potatoes over absorbent kitchen paper and keep warm until required.

Minted Sugar Snaps, Baby Gem Lettuce and Asparagus

SERVES 6

450g (1lb) sugar snap peas

2 Baby Gem lettuces, each cut into six pieces through the core

12 spears of asparagus, trimmed

30g (1oz/¹/₈ cup) butter (optional)

150ml (¹/₄ pint/⁵/₈ cup) vegetable stock or water

A small handful of mint leaves

Trim the peas and set aside.

Put the lettuce into a large casserole pot, add the butter and vegetable stock and season lightly with salt, pepper and a pinch of sugar.

Bring to the boil, reduce the heat, cover and cook over a low heat for 12–15min, or until the lettuce is nearly tender.

Add the sugar snaps and asparagus to the pot and cook for a further 4–5min, or until all the vegetables are tender. Transfer the vegetables to a serving dish.

Reduce the cooking liquid to 2–3 tbsp by boiling rapidly, season with more salt and pepper if necessary, and add the mint. Bring the dressing to the boil, pour it over the vegetables, and serve immediately.

Gooseberry Crumble

SERVES 6

675g (1¹/₂ lb) gooseberries,
washed, topped and tailed

2 tbsp redcurrant jelly

Grated zest and juice of 1 orange

3 tbsp caster sugar

For the crumble:

110g (4oz/²/₃ cup) plain flour

110g (4oz/²/₃ cup) wholemeal
flour

55g (2oz/¹/₂ cup) toasted
hazelnuts, chopped (optional)

110g (4oz/¹/₂ cup) butter

85g (3oz/¹/₂ cup) demerara sugar

Heat the oven to 190ºC (375ºF/gas mark 5).

Cut the gooseberries in half and place in a large
ovenproof pie dish.

Mix the redcurrant jelly with the orange zest and
juice and pour over the gooseberries. Sprinkle the sugar
over the fruit.

Sift the flours into a bowl and add the nuts, if using.
Cut the butter into small pieces and rub it into the flour
until it resembles coarse breadcrumbs. Add the brown
sugar and mix.

Spoon the crumble mix on top of the gooseberries
and press down lightly.

Place the ovenproof dish on a baking sheet to catch
any juices, and bake the pie on the top shelf of the oven
for 30–40min, or until the gooseberries feel soft when
pierced with a skewer and the topping is golden brown.
Remove from the oven and serve warm with
Elderflower Custard .

Elderflower Custard

Elderflowers appear in the wild during the gooseberry season. In their absence, you can infuse the milk with a handful of mint or a bay leaf.

MAKES 1LTR (1¾ PINT/4½ CUPS); SERVES 6

1ltr (1¾ pints/4½ cups) milk
8 elderflower heads (umbels)
1 vanilla pod
6 egg yolks
3–4 tbsp caster sugar
2 tsp cornflour

Place the milk, elderflower heads and vanilla pod in a large saucepan and heat gently until the milk comes to scalding point. Remove from the heat and leave to infuse for 30min.

When the milk is ready, beat the egg yolks, sugar and cornflour together until pale and smooth. Pour on the milk and stir briskly to blend it with the eggs, then return the custard to the rinsed-out saucepan.

Stir the custard over a low to medium heat until it comes back to scalding point, but don't allow it to boil. Remove from the heat and strain into a cold bowl.

Serve the custard hot, warm or cold. To prevent a crust forming, sprinkle a little caster sugar over the top.

Kentish Cherry Compôte

SERVES 6

1kg (2.2lb) cherries
55g (2oz/¼ cup) granulated sugar
150ml (¼ pint/⅝ cup) apple juice
1 vanilla pod
5 tbsp rosewater
1–2 tsp arrowroot
2 tbsp toasted flaked almonds, to serve

Remove the stones from the cherries with a pitter.

Put the sugar, apple juice and vanilla pod into a large saucepan and heat until the sugar has dissolved. Bring the liquid to a fast boil, remove it from the heat and leave to infuse for 5min.

Add the cherries to the juice and heat to simmering point, then cover with a lid and cook over a very low heat for 8–10min.

Transfer the cherries to a serving bowl with a slotted spoon.

Mix the rosewater with 1 tsp arrowroot, stir into the juice and heat until it just comes back to the boil (if it's still a little thin, add some more arrowroot). Pour the syrup over the cherries and leave to cool.

When cool, sprinkle the toasted almonds over the compôte and serve immediately. Hand the Treacle Snaps (see page 150) separately.

Treacle Snaps

110g (4oz/^{1}/$_2$ cup) butter

110g (4oz/^{2}/$_3$ cup) demerara sugar

110g (4oz/^{1}/$_2$ cup) black treacle

110g (4oz/^{2}/$_3$ cup) plain flour

A pinch of baking powder

Heat the oven to 190ºC (375ºF/gas mark 5).

Place the butter, sugar and treacle in a saucepan and heat slowly until the butter has melted and the sugar has nearly dissolved. Remove from the heat and leave to cool.

Sift the flour and baking powder into a bowl and then sift the mix into the cool treacle mixture. Stir until well blended.

Cover two baking sheets with non-stick baking parchment. Spoon the mix, a tablespoonful at a time, on to the sheet, keeping each spoonful well apart, as they will spread.

Bake the snaps for 7–8min, without allowing them to become too dark. Remove from the oven and cool for 2–3min, or until pliable, but not soft.

Lightly oil a rolling pin and press the treacle snaps around it to form a curved shape. Cool on a wire rack. If the snaps become too brittle to bend, put them back into the oven for a few seconds to soften them, and then try again.

Serve with Kentish Cherry Compôte. If you have any snaps left over, they will keep in an airtight container for a day or so.

FAMILY CELEBRATIONS

The summer months are usually a busy time for the family. Weddings and christenings may be celebrated at any time of the year, but traditionally christenings, dedications, baptisms and confirmation took place in late spring and weddings during the month of June.

Many christenings are part of a Sunday family service: the baby is welcomed into the church family when many of the congregation are present. To celebrate this special family occasion, we have a Sunday buffet for a christening feast. The recipes will serve ten, so they are perfect if you have a larger than usual group to feed.

If you want a christening cake you can either choose the Summer Celebration Cake or for a more traditional cake – the Rich Fruit Cake recipe (see page 30) is ideal. Traditionally the top tier of a wedding cake is set aside for the first baby's christening; all you need to do is re-marzipan and ice the cake.

The recipe ideas for this occasion are not designed to go together as a complete menu; you may choose one or two main courses from the list and add your own selection of salads and potatoes or rice as an accompaniment. The puddings are very seasonal; if you want chocolate, there are plenty of ideas to choose from elsewhere in the book.

CHRISTENING BUFFET

ALL RECIPES SERVE 10

Hot dishes:
Salmon, Red Pepper and Fennel Florentine
Chicken and Tarragon Fusilli Gratin

Cold dishes:
Marinated Duck and Summer Vegetable Salad
Olive and Basil Penne Salad
Frozen Coffee and Raspberry Meringue Roulade
Apricot, Peach and Passion Fruit Terrine

Serve a single-estate Soave Classico Superiore to complement the Mediterranean flavours of this buffet.

Salmon, Red Pepper and Fennel Florentine

To save time, this dish can be prepared in advance to the stage marked * and assembled and reheated when required.

SERVES 10

2kg (4.4lb) spinach

5 tbsp extra virgin olive oil

$^1/_2$ tsp ground nutmeg

900g (2lb) salmon fillet, skinned and pin-boned

A slice of lemon

300ml ($^1/_2$ pint/1$^1/_4$ cup) fish stock

3 red peppers, finely sliced

1 head of Florence fennel, finely sliced

2 cloves garlic, crushed (optional)

$^1/_2$ tsp paprika

250ml (8fl oz/1 cup) double cream

250ml (8fl oz/1 cup) Greek yoghurt

110g (4oz/1 cup) freshly grated Parmesan cheese

4 egg yolks

Wash the spinach very thoroughly and tear into shreds.

Heat 1 tbsp of the olive oil in a frying pan and season with a little nutmeg, salt and pepper. Add half of the spinach at a time and cook over a very high heat until wilted. Transfer to a plate, chop finely and pat dry with absorbent paper, if necessary. Set aside.

Cut the salmon into 4cm (1$^1/_2$in) pieces. Place them in a large saucepan, add the lemon slice and stock, and poach over a very low heat for 5–6min, or until the fish is just cooked – don't overcook, as it will dry further on reheating. Transfer the fish to a plate and leave to drain.

Heat the remaining olive oil and sauté the red peppers and fennel for 4–5min, add the garlic, if using, and the paprika. Continue to cook until the peppers and fennel are soft and beginning to break up. Season with salt, pepper and sugar and leave to cool.*

To assemble the dish, heat the oven to 180°C (350°F/gas mark 4). Place the spinach at the bottom of a large shallow ovenproof dish. Mix the salmon and red peppers together and check the seasoning. Spoon the mixture over the spinach.

Mix the cream, yoghurt, cheese and egg yolks together, season with salt, pepper and nutmeg and pour over the salmon.

Bake for 20–25min, or until the dish is piping hot and the yoghurt is set – be careful not to overcook it – and serve.

Chicken and Tarragon Fusilli Gratin

This dish can be prepared in advance to the stage marked *, but if you do so, assemble it only when all the components are chilled.

SERVES 10

1 x 2kg (4.4lb) roasting chicken

1 onion, finely sliced

1 carrot, finely sliced

4 cloves garlic; 2 peeled and 2 crushed

2 bay leaves

2 tbsp olive oil

450g (1lb) cherry tomatoes, cut in half

2 sticks of celery, finely sliced

3 tbsp freshly chopped tarragon

675g (1½lbs/5 cups) fusilli

300ml (½ pint/1¼ cups) crème fraîche

6 tbsp fresh breadcrumbs

3 tbsp freshly grated Gruyère cheese

Remove any fine feathers from the chicken and place it in a large casserole pot with the onion and carrot. Cover with water and add the bay leaves and whole crushed garlic. Bring to the boil, then reduce the heat and poach for 1–1¼ hours, or until the chicken is cooked.

Remove the chicken from the pot and take the meat off the bones, discarding any skin or fat. Cut the meat into large pieces.

Heat the olive oil in a saucepan and cook the cherry tomatoes and celery for 2–3min, then add the remaining garlic and half of the chopped tarragon. Cook for a further 1–2min. Remove from the heat, season to taste with salt and pepper and leave to cool.*

Cook the fusilli in boiling, salted water for 8–10min, or until al dente. Drain and leave to dry. Transfer the pasta to a large bowl, add the crème fraîche and the rest of the tarragon, and season to taste with salt and pepper.

Heat the oven to 190°C (375°F/gas mark 5).

Mix the cold chicken with the cold tomato mixture and the pasta. Check the seasoning and transfer to a large gratin dish.

Mix the breadcrumbs and cheese together and sprinkle over the chicken. Bake the gratin for 25–30min, or until piping hot. Serve immediately.

Marinated Duck
and Summer Vegetable Salad

This dish can be prepared well in advance, but should only be assembled when you are ready to serve. Chicken, or aubergine for vegetarians, can be easily substituted for the duck.

SERVES 10

6 duck breasts, skin removed

For the marinade:

1 large onion, finely sliced

4 tbsp hoisin sauce

3 tbsp dark soy sauce

3 tbsp plum jam

2 tbsp sesame oil

2 tsp freshly grated root ginger

A little sunflower oil

For the dressing:

4 tbsp sunflower oil

1 tbsp coarse grain mustard

3–4 tbsp rice wine vinegar

1 tbsp light brown sugar

340g (12oz) green beans

225g (8oz) young asparagus spears

450g (1lb) baby corn

450g (1lb) baby carrots

20 small new potatoes

8 spring onions, thickly sliced, and 2 tbsp toasted sesame seeds, to serve

Place the duck breasts in a shallow dish. Mix together the ingredients for the marinade and pour it over the duck. Season with freshly ground black pepper. Cover with cling film and marinate in the refrigerator for 2 hours.

Heat the oven to 220°C (425°F/gas mark 7).

Pat the duck breasts dry. Heat a little sunflower oil in a frying pan, add the duck and cook very briskly for 1min on each side. Arrange the duck breasts in a single layer in a roasting tin. Pour the marinade into a pan and bring to the boil, then cook for 5–6min, or until reduced and sticky. Pour the marinade over the duck.

Roast for 15min, or until the duck is thoroughly cooked, to a maximum of 20min. Transfer the duck to a plate and leave to cool.

Pour the marinade from the roasting tin into a bowl and add the dressing ingredients. Whisk together until well mixed and set aside.

Blanch the beans, asparagus, baby corn and carrots for 1–2min, then drain and refresh them under running cold water, before drying on absorbent kitchen paper. Cook the potatoes in plenty of boiling, salted water for 10–12min, or until tender, and drain.

To serve, place the cooked vegetables, spring onions and sesame seeds in a large serving bowl, pour over the dressing and season to taste with salt and pepper. Carve the duck into thin strips and toss them into the salad.

Olive and Basil
Penne Salad

SERVES 10

675g (1¼lb/5 cups) tri-coloured penne

1 tbsp sunflower oil

5 tbsp olive tapenade

150ml (¼ pint/⅝ cup) soured cream

A large handful of basil leaves

Lemon juice, to taste

1 tbsp caster sugar

140g (5oz) prosciutto or ham, cut into strips

55g (2oz/⅓ cup) toasted pine nuts

Sprigs of basil, to garnish

110g (4oz/½ cup) mixed olives, pitted

Cook the pasta in plenty of boiling, salted water for 10–12min, or until al dente, then drain and transfer to a large bowl. Add the sunflower oil and tapenade, and season to taste with salt and pepper.

Place the soured cream and basil in a small saucepan, bring to the boil and simmer for 1–2min, or until the basil is soft. Remove from the heat, pour into a liquidizer and whizz to form a purée. Add lemon juice and sugar to taste and season with salt and pepper.

Toss in the prepared prosciutto, pine nuts and olive and basil dressing, then spoon into a large serving dish and garnish with the sprigs of basil and olives. Serve immediately.

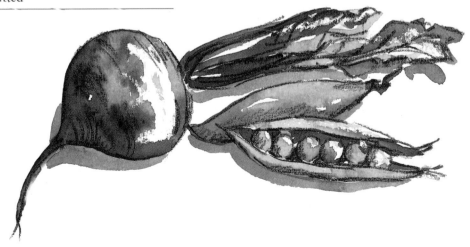

Frozen Coffee and Raspberry Meringue Roulade

SERVES 10

6 egg whites

340g (12oz/2 cups) icing sugar

1 tbsp cold strong coffee

1 tsp lemon juice

2 tsp cornflour

For the filling:

300ml ($1/2$ pint/$1^1/4$ cups) Greek yoghurt

225g (8oz/$1^1/2$ cups) fresh raspberries

1 tbsp crème de cassis (optional)

Grated dark chocolate, to serve

Heat the oven to 150°C (300°F/gas mark 2). Prepare a Swiss roll case measuring 40x25cm (16x10in) by cutting two pieces of non-stick baking parchment, placing them one on top of the other and folding the sides up. Secure the corners with paper clips.

To make the meringue, place the egg whites into a large dry glass bowl, set over a saucepan of simmering water (don't allow the water to touch the bowl). Whisk the egg whites until frothy. Add the icing sugar, a spoonful at a time, until it is all whisked in. Continue to whisk for 8–10min until the mixture is very thick, glossy and holds its shape.

Add the coffee, lemon juice and cornflour and fold in gently. Spoon the mixture into the prepared case, spreading it flat. Bake for 40–45min, or until the top of the roulade is set and crisp.

Remove from the oven and cover the top with a piece of dampened non-stick baking parchment. Leave to cool for 30min.

Turn the roulade on to another piece of non-stick baking parchment and remove the case very carefully. Spread the yoghurt over the surface, scatter the raspberries over the top and splash a little cassis over. Roll the roulade lengthways into a Swiss roll shape, using the baking parchment to help – it will crack a little. Keep it enclosed in the paper and wrap in tin foil. Freeze for 2 hours.

To serve the roulade, remove the foil and paper, sprinkle the dark chocolate over the top and place in the refrigerator for 15min before cutting into slices.

Apricot, Peach and Passion Fruit Terrine

SERVES 10

450g (1lb) apricots

140g (5oz/⅝ cup) caster sugar

150ml (¼ pint/⅝ cup) dry white wine

150ml (¼ pint/⅝ cup) orange juice

1 vanilla pod

3 level tbsp powdered gelatine

125ml (4fl oz/½ cup) cold water

12 ripe passion fruit

8 ripe peaches

Sprigs of mint and a few strawberries, cut in half, to serve

Cut the apricots in half and stone them. Place them in a large saucepan with the sugar, wine and orange juice. Bring to the boil and add the vanilla pod, then reduce the heat and cook over a low heat until the fruit is soft. Remove the vanilla pod.

Soak the gelatine in the water for 5min.

Transfer the cooked apricots and all the juice to a food processor and whizz together to form a smooth purée. Add a little more sugar, to taste.

Warm the gelatine until it's completely dissolved and clear, then add it to the apricot purée mixture and stir well. Set aside to cool.

In the meantime, cut the passion fruit in half. Scoop out the seeds and juice and stir into the apricot purée.

Blanch the peaches in boiling water for 30 seconds, then put into a bowl of cold water. Peel away the skin and stone them, then cut into small 1cm (½in) chunks. Add the peaches to the cold fruit purée and pour into a lightly oiled 1.5ltr (3 pint) loaf tin. Cover and chill for 4 hours, or until set.

To serve the terrine, loosen it from the tin by immersing the tin in hot water. Turn the terrine on to a large glass plate and decorate with the mint and strawberries.

Importantly, a child's birthday is a great opportunity for celebration. The recipe selection is simple, reasonably healthy and easy to prepare. For birthday cakes, there are several suitable ideas to choose from in other sections of the book.

SERVES 15

Pizza Crumpets
Baked Marmite Potato Wedges
Filo Sausage Rolls
Strawberry Ripple Yoghurt Milkshake
Crocs and Sharks Jellies

Pizza Crumpets

MAKES 15

15 crumpets
1 onion, finely chopped
1 tbsp sunflower oil
400g (14oz/2 cups) tinned chopped tomatoes
2 tbsp Worcestershire sauce
1 tbsp soft dark brown sugar
1 tsp dried or fresh oregano
110g (4oz/1 cup) grated mozzarella cheese
110g (4oz/1 cup) sliced pepperoni (optional)

Heat the oven to 190°C (375°F/gas mark 5).

To make the topping, heat the oil in a frying pan and cook the onion for 7–10min, or until soft. Add the tomatoes, Worcestershire sauce, brown sugar and oregano. Season to taste with salt and black pepper and simmer over a medium heat for 12–15min, or until reduced to a thick pulp.

Put the crumpets on a baking sheet and bake for 5min.

Spread the tomato mixture on to the warm crumpets, sprinkle the cheese over and arrange the pepperoni slices on top. Bake for 15–20min, or until the cheese has melted and the top is beginning to brown. Cut the pizza crumpets in half and serve.

Baked Marmite Potato Wedges

SERVES 15

12 small baking potatoes

1 tbsp sunflower oil

1 tbsp Marmite (yeast extract)

150ml (¼ pint/⅝ cup) tomato juice

Heat the oven to 200°C (400°F/gas mark 6).

Scrub the potatoes and cut each in half lengthways, then each half into 3–4 wedges.

Put the oil into a bowl, add the potato wedges and toss them around so that each has a light coating. Season with a little freshly ground black pepper.

Arrange the potato wedges on a baking sheet and bake for 35–40min, or until lightly browned and soft.

Warm the Marmite and tomato juice together in a small saucepan and brush over the potato wedges. Bake for a further 5min and serve warm.

Filo Sausage Rolls

MAKES 30

450g (1lb) sausage meat

1 tbsp chopped herbs such as parsley or sage

4 spring onions, finely chopped

5 sheets of filo pastry

55g (2oz/¼ cup) butter, melted

1 egg, beaten

Poppy seeds, to decorate (optional)

Tomato ketchup, to serve

Heat the oven to 200°C (400°F/gas mark 6).

Mix the sausage meat, herbs and spring onions together and season with salt and black pepper. Shape the meat into 5 sausages the length of a sheet of filo pastry and about 2.5cm (1in) in diameter.

Brush each sheet of filo pastry with melted butter and roll it up lengthways, enclosing a sausage. Trim the ends of each roll and cut into 4cm (1½in) lengths.

Arrange the sausage rolls on a baking sheet and brush with a little beaten egg, then sprinkle the poppy seeds over the top and bake on the top shelf of the oven for 12–15min, or until the pastry is golden brown and the sausage meat is cooked. Transfer to a wire rack to cool slightly before serving.

Serve with a bowl of tomato ketchup as a dip.

Strawberry Ripple Yoghurt Milkshake

This milkshake will keep in the refrigerator for 3 hours.

SERVES 15

1.5ltr (3 pints/6 cups) semi-skimmed milk

6 ripe bananas

Juice of ½ lemon

300ml (½ pint/1¼ cups) natural yoghurt

100ml (3½fl oz/¾ cup) runny honey

1 tsp vanilla essence

450g (1lb/2½ cups) strawberries

2–3 tbsp icing sugar

Crushed ice, to serve (optional)

Pour half of the milk into a liquidizer, add three bananas and whizz together to form a purée, then transfer to a large bowl or jug. Do the same with the remaining milk and bananas and add to the first batch. Stir in the lemon juice, natural yoghurt, honey and vanilla essence. Chill until required.

Place the strawberries in a bowl, add the sugar and crush the strawberries with a fork so that the fruit is broken up, but not puréed. Chill until required.

To serve, spoon some of the strawberry mixture into the bottom of individual cups (transparent if possible) and top with milkshake. Briefly stir to create a ripple effect and add a little crushed ice, if desired.

Crocs and Sharks Jellies

SERVES 15

1.5ltr (3 pints/6 cups) clear fruit juice, such as apple, or diluted elderflower cordial

3 tbsp gelatine

Juice of ½ lemon

A selection of fruit gums such as crocodiles, sharks, spiders or teddy bears

Paper jelly moulds

Warm 150ml (¼ pint) of the apple juice until tepid and stir into the remaining juice.

Pour 150ml (¼ pint) of the warm juice into a bowl and add the lemon juice and gelatine. Leave to soak for 5min, or until the gelatine is spongy.

Dissolve the gelatine over a very low heat until completely liquid, but not very hot, then stir into the apple juice. Leave to cool for 15min.

Arrange a few fruit gums in the base of each paper jelly mould and pour the cooled apple juice over the top. Cover and chill for 2 hours to allow the jelly to set.

WEDDING CELEBRATIONS

Many people would never consider preparing their own wedding feast. However, an afternoon tea with finger food is a wonderful way to celebrate a smaller wedding. Most of the recipes chosen can be prepared some way in advance, but you will need to enlist someone's help to assemble and present your food, and of course to help serve.

Finger food for this type of occasion needs to be plentiful, but also exciting. Each recipe will give thirty portions, but you may prefer to choose a smaller selection of recipes. For a reception lasting several hours, count on at least fifteen to eighteen pieces per person.

The wedding cake is a variation on a theme. The classic French wedding gâteau – Croquembouche – is a tower of choux pastry with a traditional crème patisserie to fill. If you want something a little more traditional, the Rich Fruit Cake recipe (see page 30) is an excellent base.

FINGER FOOD FOR AN AFTERNOON RECEPTION

Smoked Fish and Caper Pâté on Corn Pancakes
Roast Vegetable and Roquefort Tartlets
Crab, Ginger and Avocado Croustades
Tapenade Bruschetta with Tomato Salsa
Prosciutto and Basil Grissini Sticks
Pastrami, Rocket and Mozarella Rolls
Hot Chicken and Pesto Filo Parcels
Hot Pork Goujons with Chilli
Strawberry Shortbread Hearts
Grape and Cherry Caramels
Summer Cooler

TRADITIONAL FRENCH WEDDING CAKE

Three-chocolate Croquembouche

A celebration wouldn't be complete without bubbly, and a New Zealand sparkling white, such as Lindauer, has just the right light touch.

Smoked Fish and Caper Pâté on Corn Pancakes

The pancake batter for this recipe has to be made 1 hour before the pancakes are cooked. The cooked pancakes can be stored in an airtight container for up to 2 days before assembly.

MAKES 30

225g (8oz/1 cup) canned sweetcorn kernels, roughly chopped

110g (4oz/^{2}/$_3$ cup) plain flour

1 tsp baking powder

1 tsp grated nutmeg

^{1}/$_2$ tsp cayenne pepper

55g (2oz/^{1}/$_2$ cup) fine cornmeal

250ml (8fl oz/1 cup) buttermilk

3 eggs

1 tbsp corn oil

For the paté:

110g (4oz) smoked salmon

110g (4oz) smoked trout

110g (4oz) smoked halibut

2 tbsp capers

1 red onion, finely chopped

1 tbsp finely chopped parsley

225g (8oz/1^1/$_2$ cups) low fat cream cheese

1 tsp anchovy essence

1 tbsp creamed horseradish

Lemon juice to taste

Sprigs of dill, to garnish

To make the pancake batter, pat the chopped sweetcorn dry with absorbent kitchen paper. Sift the flour, baking powder, spices and cornmeal into a large bowl, and make a well in the centre. Mix together 3–4 tbsp of the buttermilk, the eggs and the oil, and pour into the middle of the well. Stir the liquid around, gradually incorporating the flour and add more buttermilk as the mixture begins to thicken. Once all the flour is incorporated, add any remaining buttermilk and the sweetcorn. Cover and chill for 1 hour.

Meanwhile, make the pâté. Finely chop the smoked fish, place it in a bowl with the remaining ingredients and beat together until well mixed. Add lemon juice, salt and freshly ground black pepper to taste. Set aside until required.

To make the corn pancakes, brush a large frying pan with a thin layer of oil and heat it until a haze is produced. Ladle small spoonfuls of batter into the frying pan to form rounds approximately 5cm (2in) in diameter. Fry on each side for 2–3min or until lightly browned. Transfer pancakes to a wire rack and continue to cook the remaining batter.

To assemble with the topping, fill a piping bag fitted with a 2cm (^{3}/$_4$ in) plain nozzle with the pâté, pipe a swirl on to the corn pancakes and top each with a sprig of dill. Chill until required.

Roast Vegetable and Roquefort Tartlets

MAKES 30

1 courgette

2 red peppers

1 large red onion

2 tbsp extra virgin olive oil

1 clove garlic, crushed

A pinch of cayenne pepper

6 sheets of filo pastry

225g (8oz) baby asparagus, spears only, blanched

2 tbsp chopped flat leaf parsley

110g (4oz/¾ cup) Roquefort cheese, crumbled, to serve

Heat the oven to 200°C (400°F/gas mark 6).

Dice the courgette, red pepper and red onion into 2cm (¾ in) chunks. Toss in the oil, garlic and cayenne pepper and season to taste with salt and pepper.

Roast in the oven for 15–20min, turning the vegetables over every 5–7min – they should be lightly coloured and cooked. Once cooked, lift on to a plate and remove excess oil with absorbent paper.

For the tartlets: Brush each sheet of filo with some oil, stack two sheets one on top of the other and cut into 5cm (2in) squares. Lay the pastry squares into small tartlet tins to form a tartlet. Bake in the oven for 8–10min or until light golden brown and crisp. Lift on to a wire rack to cool.

To assemble, pile the vegetables into the middle of the filo tartlets, arrange an asparagus spear on top and sprinkle with parsley and cheese. Serve immediately.

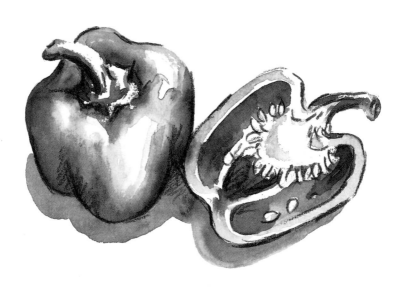

Crab, Ginger and Avocado Croustades

Make the topping and assemble these just before serving, if possible, as avocado quickly becomes discoloured.

MAKES 30

For the croustades:

10 slices of medium sliced brown bread

A little unsalted butter, melted

For the filling:

450g (1lb) good quality white crabmeat

3 tsp freshly grated ginger

5 tbsp mayonnaise

$^1/_2$ tsp cayenne pepper

2 spring onions, finely chopped

Lime juice, to taste

For the topping:

1 ripe avocado, peeled and finely diced

2 tomatoes, peeled and diced

A squeeze of lime juice

Heat the oven to 180ºC (350ºF/gas mark 4).

Roll the bread a little thinner with a rolling pin, then, using a 5cm (2in) pastry cutter, cut out rounds of bread and brush each with some melted butter. Press the rounds into patty tin moulds and bake for 8–10min, or until crisp and lightly toasted.

Check the crabmeat very carefully and remove any broken shell. Mix together the ingredients for the filling and season to taste with lime juice, salt and pepper.

Just before serving, mix together the ingredients for the topping and season with salt, pepper and a little sugar. Add the lime juice to help prevent discolouration.

Spoon the filling generously into the croustade cases, top with the avocado mixture and serve.

Tapenade Bruschetta with Tomato Salsa

MAKES 30

3 very thin baguettes

2–3 tbsp olive oil

Finely ground sea salt

For the tapenade:

110g (4oz/1 cup) black olives (preferably kalamata), stoned

110g (4oz/1 cup) Spanish green olives (preferably Manzanilla), stoned

4 anchovy fillets

2 cloves garlic, crushed

3 tbsp extra virgin olive oil

1 tbsp capers

For the salsa:

8 tomatoes, cut in half, deseeded and chopped

2 tbsp sundried tomato paste

1 tbsp chopped mint

1 red onion, finely chopped

1–2 tbsp olive oil

1 tbsp dark brown sugar

Heat the oven to 200°C (400°F/gas mark 6).

Cut the bread into slices about 1cm (1/2in) thick. Arrange on a baking sheet, drizzle the oil and sprinkle the sea salt over the top.

Bake for 8–10min, or until lightly browned, then transfer to a wire rack to cool.

Place all the ingredients for the tapenade in a food processor and whizz together to form a smooth paste, then season with salt and freshly ground black pepper.

Mix the ingredients for the salsa together and season with salt and freshly ground black pepper. Spread a generous layer of tapenade on to the bruschetta and spoon a little salsa on top. Serve immediately.

Prosciutto and Basil Grissini Sticks

MAKES 30

30 small grissini sticks

A little extra virgin olive oil

15 slices of prosciutto

55g (2oz) Parmesan cheese, freshly grated

30 small basil leaves, shredded

250ml (8fl oz/1 cup) Greek yoghurt

2 tbsp chopped chives

Dip the end of each grissini stick in olive oil and set aside.

Trim the prosciutto, removing any excess fat, and brush with a little oil. Sprinkle a little cheese and a few basil leaves on top of each slice. Cut each slice in two.

Carefully wrap a strip of prosciutto around each grissini, with the cheese and basil on the inside.

Mix together the yoghurt and chives and season to taste.

To serve, arrange the sticks in a large jug and hand the dip separately.

Pastrami, Rocket and Mozzarella Rolls

MAKES 30

30 small slices of pastrami

2 tbsp creamed horseradish

200g (7oz) mozzarella cheese, cut into finger-length strips

A bunch of wild rocket, washed and long stalks trimmed

300ml (½ pint/1¼ cups) mayonnaise

4 cloves of garlic (or according to taste), crushed

3 tbsp chopped flat-leaf parsley

Radicchio lettuce, to serve

Lay the pastrami on a clean work surface and spread each slice with a little horseradish. Arrange a couple of strips of mozzarella along the bottom of each slice and add a few rocket leaves. Season with freshly ground black pepper. Roll each strip up, cover with greaseproof paper and chill until required.

To make the aïoli dip, mix the mayonnaise, garlic and flat-leaf parsley together and season to taste.

To serve, cut the pastrami into 4cm (1½in) lengths and arrange on a bed of radicchio. Hand the aïoli dip separately.

Hot Chicken and Pesto Filo Parcels

MAKES 30

450g (1lb) cooked chicken or smoked turkey

110g (4oz/1 cup) pine nuts, toasted

4 sundried tomatoes, chopped

A large handful of basil leaves

2 cloves garlic, crushed

55g (2oz/³/4 cup) freshly grated Parmesan cheese

5 tbsp olive oil, plus extra to brush

8 sheets filo pastry

Basil leaves, to serve

Remove any skin and bones from the chicken and cut the meat into shreds. Place in a bowl with the sundried tomatoes and half of the pine nuts, mix together, cover and chill until needed.

To make the pesto, place the basil leaves, garlic, cheese and remaining pine nuts in a food processor and whizz to form a purée. With the motor of the machine running, add 5 tbsp olive oil in a thin stream until the mixture is emulsified. Season to taste with salt and ground black pepper. Stir the pesto into the chicken mixture and chill until required.

Heat the oven to 200ºC (400ºF/gas mark 6).

Brush the sheets of filo pastry with olive oil, fold each sheet in half and cut it into four squares.

Place a spoonful of the chicken filling in the centre of each square and draw the edges up to form a parcel. Brush the outside of the filo parcels with a little extra oil, arrange on a baking sheet and bake for 12–15min, or until the pastry is golden brown and the filling piping hot.

Once cooked, transfer the parcels to absorbent kitchen paper to remove any excess oil. Arrange a pile of parcels on a serving plate, garnish with the basil and serve.

Hot Pork Goujons with Chilli

SERVES 30

450g (1lb) pork fillet

4 tbsp sweet chilli sauce

2 tbsp dark soy sauce

2 tbsp soft dark brown sugar

1 tbsp sesame oil

200–250ml (8fl oz / 1 cup) sweet chilli sauce

4 spring onions, finely sliced

1 tbsp sesame seeds

A little oil

Sprigs of coriander and cocktail sticks, to serve

Trim the pork fillet of any sinew and cut into finger-length strips. Place in a bowl with the sweet chilli sauce, soy sauce, sugar and sesame oil, and season well with black pepper. Cover and refrigerate for 8 hours.

Meanwhile, make the dipping sauce. Mix the sweet chilli sauce and spring onions together and set aside until required.

When the pork is ready, add the sesame seeds to the bowl and mix in well, then season with a little salt. Heat a splash of oil in a wok, add a few strips of pork at a time and stir-fry until brown and sticky. Transfer cooked meat to a plate and continue until all the pork is cooked.

To serve, place the hot goujons on a large serving dish and garnish with sprigs of coriander. Hand the dipping sauce and cocktail sticks separately.

Strawberry Shortbread Hearts

These heart-shaped biscuits can be made a few days in advance and kept in an airtight container.

MAKES 30

170g (6oz/1 cup) plain flour

55g (2oz/½ cup) ground rice

170g (6oz/¾ cup) unsalted butter

Grated zest of 2 lemons

85g (3oz/⅜ cup) caster sugar

Icing sugar, to dust

Strawberries, to serve

Sift the flour and ground rice into a bowl. Cut the butter into small pieces and rub into the flour until it resembles coarse breadcrumbs.

Add the lemon zest and sugar and stir in, then knead the mixture, it comes together to form a smooth dough.

Cut the dough into quarters. Roll out each piece to approximately ½cm (⅛in) thickness and cut out biscuits with a small heart-shaped cutter. Arrange the biscuits on a baking sheet, lined with non-stick baking parchment, and chill for 1 hour.

Heat the oven to 180°C (350°F/gas mark 4).

Bake the biscuits on the second shelf of the oven for 12–15min, or until light golden brown. Transfer to a wire rack to cool, then dust with icing sugar.

Keep the hearts in an airtight box until required. To serve, arrange the hearts on a large serving plate and garnish with strawberries.

Grape and Cherry Caramels

It is worth making a large quantity of caramel – you may not use it all, but it will give you plenty to play with. Make these within two hours of serving, if possible.

MAKES 30

30–40 mixed dark red cherries and grapes, stalks on, washed and dried

225g (8oz/1 cup) caster sugar

150ml (1/4 pint/5/8 cup) hot water

1 vanilla pod, split

You will need a bowl of iced water when dipping the fruit in caramel.

To make the caramel, place the sugar and hot water in a large saucepan and heat until the sugar has dissolved. Add the vanilla pod, bring to the boil and simmer for 10min. Remove the vanilla pod and continue to boil the syrup until it turns a dark toffee colour.

Leave the caramel to cool for 2–3min and then work quickly to dip the cherries. Hold the fruit by the stalk and dip it into the cooling caramel, taking care not to burn your fingers. Keep a bowl of iced water at hand, just in case you get caramel on your skin.

If the caramel begins to get too thick and will no longer coat the cherries evenly, put it back over a low heat for 1–2min to thin it down.

Once dipped, place the cherries and grapes on a sheet of non-stick baking parchment to set. They should be eaten within 2 hours, as the caramel will begin to soften if left too long.

Three-chocolate Croquembouche

This cake needs to be assembled shortly before it is required. However the component parts can be prepared up to the stage marked * a little in advance.

Makes a cake 30cm (12in) high; requires a 30cm (12in) silver cake board.

250g (9oz/1^1/8 cups) unsalted butter

675ml (23fl oz/2^7/8 cups) cold water

340g (12oz/2^1/2 cups) plain flour, sifted

9 eggs

For the milk chocolate cream:

750ml (1^1/4 pint/3 cups) milk

450g (1lb/2 cups) milk chocolate, grated

7 egg yolks

70g (2^1/2oz/^{1}/2 cup) caster sugar

70g (2^1/2oz/^{1}/2 cup) cornflour

4^1/2 heaped tbsp plain flour

1 tbsp strong cold coffee

For the dark chocolate topping:

675g (1^1/2 lbs/3 cups) dark chocolate, chopped

110g (4oz/^{1}/2 cup) butter

100ml (3^1/2fl oz/^{7}/8 cup) brandy

200g (7oz/^{7}/8 cup) white chocolate, shaved into curls with a peeler, to garnish

To make the choux pastry, place the butter and water in a saucepan over a low heat and melt the butter. Working quickly, bring it to a fast boil, add the flour, immediately draw the pan off the heat and beat furiously until the mixture just comes to a smooth paste – don't overbeat it. Spread the paste on to a plate to cool.

Heat the oven to 200°C (400°F/gas mark 6).

Beat the eggs and add them, a splash at a time, to the cool paste mixture, beating well between each addition. Continue to add the eggs until a very smooth, glossy mixture is formed that holds its shape – you may not need all the egg.

Fill a piping bag fitted with a 1cm (^{1}/2in) nozzle with the pastry. Pipe 2cm (^{3}/4in) rounds on to a baking sheet lined with non-stick baking parchment. The pastry will spread so don't pipe the buns too closely together. Bake on the top shelf of the oven for 12–15min, or until the buns are well risen and a rich golden brown – don't remove them until they look dark enough, as they will shrink. Once cooked, turn each bun over and make a small hole in the base to allow the steam to escape, then return to the oven for 1–2min. Transfer to a wire rack to cool.

To make the milk chocolate cream, place the chocolate and 150ml (^{1}/4 pint/^{7}/8 cup) of the milk in a saucepan over a very low heat and stir until a smooth cream forms.

Beat the egg yolks, sugar and flours together with a little of the remaining milk to form a smooth paste. Add all of the remaining milk, the coffee and the chocolate cream to the paste and stir well to blend. Return the mixture to a clean saucepan and stir over a low heat until the custard thickens – it will go lumpy initially, but will become smooth if you keep stirring over the heat. When it's smooth, bring to the boil for 1–2min, then set aside to cool.

To make the dark chocolate topping, place the chocolate, butter and brandy in a large glass bowl, set over a saucepan of simmering water (don't allow the water to touch the bowl). Stir until the chocolate has just melted, then remove and set aside to cool.*

To assemble the cake, pipe the milk chocolate filling into the choux buns to fill them generously. Dip each one in the dark chocolate topping and arrange in a single layer on the cake board. Pack them neatly so that they will stack well as the tower becomes higher. Keep filling and stacking the choux buns until the cake is about 30cm(12in) high. Once arranged, drizzle with the remaining chocolate topping. Sprinkle the white chocolate curls over the croquembouche and keep it cool until required – it should hold its shape for a few hours. Good luck!

Summer Cooler

Substitute a non-vintage champagne or sparkling wine for the lemonade if preferred, or serve both versions.

SERVES 10

2ltr (3^1/$_2$ pints/7^1/$_2$ cups) lemonade, chilled

150ml (^{1}/$_4$ pint/^{5}/$_8$ cup) crème de cassis or blackcurrant cordial

4–5 tbsp rosewater

200g (7oz) raspberries

200g (7oz) blueberries

Lavender flowers, a handful of rose petals (preferably red), a few sprigs of mint and crushed ice, to serve

Pour the lemonade into a large jug with the crème de cassis (or blackcurrant cordial), rosewater and fruit. Stir together and leave to chill for 15min.

Scatter a handful of lavender flowers, rose petals and mint on top, and serve with plenty of ice.

WEDDING ANNIVERSARIES

Summer is also a perfect time to celebrate wedding anniversaries. Be it a first (paper) anniversary, fifth (wood), tenth (tin), twenty-fifth (silver) or fiftieth (golden), this can be a great family get-together, often involving several generations.

WEDDING ANNIVERSARY LUNCH

SERVES 10

Baked Salmon with Horseradish Tzatziki
Roast Beet and Rocket Salad
Wild and Brown Basmati Rice Salad
Stone Fruit and Summer Berry Pudding

Serve a peach-like Viognier from Lagarde in Argentina.

Baked Salmon
with Horseradish Tzatziki

SERVES 10

1 tbsp sunflower oil

8 spring onions, finely sliced

1 tbsp chopped fresh mint

1 tbsp runny honey

3kg (6½ lb) salmon, filleted, pin-boned, but not skinned

6 cloves garlic, unpeeled

1 onion, thinly sliced

8 bay leaves

5 tbsp white wine

8 black peppercorns

4 sprigs of mint

For the tzatziki:

2 tbsp fresh mint, finely chopped

1 tbsp creamed horseradish

300ml (½ pint/1¼ cups) Greek yoghurt

1 tbsp chopped capers

Sprigs of mint, to garnish

Heat the oven to 180°C (350°F/gas mark 4). Lightly oil a large sheet of aluminium foil.

Heat the oil in a frying pan, add the spring onions and fry over a medium heat for 3–4min, or until soft. Transfer the onions to a bowl and leave to cool, then add the mint and honey and season to taste with salt and black pepper.

Place one of the fish fillets, skin side down, on the tin foil. Spread the cold onion mixture over the fish and place the second fillet, skin side uppermost, on top. Scatter the garlic cloves, sliced onion and bay leaves around and over the fish, and fold the foil up the sides of the fish. Pour on the wine and a splash of water, add the peppercorns and mint, close the foil loosely and bake the fish for 30–40min, or until it becomes opaque.

Meanwhile, mix the ingredients for the tzatziki together, season to taste with salt and black pepper and chill until required.

Remove the cooked salmon from the foil and arrange on a large dish. Garnish with the sprigs of mint and serve hot or cold, with the sauce.

Roast Beet and Rocket Salad

SERVES 10

10 medium uncooked beetroot

300ml ($^1/_2$ pint/1$^1/_4$ cups) boiling water

2 sprigs of thyme

For the dressing:

2 tbsp hazelnut oil

2 tbsp grapeseed oil

1 tsp soft dark brown sugar

1–2 tbsp sherry vinegar

1 tsp grain mustard

140g (5oz) rocket leaves, to serve

Heat the oven to 180ºC (350ºF/gas mark 4).

Put the raw beetroot in a roasting tin and add the water and thyme leaves. Bake for 50–60min, or until the beetroot is tender. Remove the thyme and discard.

Meanwhile, make the dressing. Place all the ingredients in a bowl and whisk until emulsified. Season to taste with salt and freshly ground black pepper.

Peel and cut the cooked beetroot into chunks and transfer to a serving dish. Add the rocket and dressing and toss the salad. Season again with salt and freshly ground pepper, to taste, and serve immediately.

Wild and Brown Basmati Rice Salad

SERVES 10

225g (8oz/1¼ cups) wild rice

340g (12oz/2½ cups) brown basmati rice

1.75ltr (3 pints/6 cups) vegetable or chicken stock

For the dressing:

110g (4oz/⅔ cup) sultanas

2 tbsp sesame oil

1 tbsp grapeseed oil

1 tbsp runny honey

2 tbsp rice wine vinegar

110g (4oz/1 cup) roasted cashew nuts, chopped

1 red onion, finely chopped

½ cucumber, deseeded and diced

2 tbsp chopped chives

Wash the rice in plenty of cold running water for 30 seconds. Place in a large saucepan, cover with the stock and season with salt and black pepper. Bring to the boil, lower the heat and simmer for 30–35min, or until the rice is cooked and the liquid is absorbed. If the liquid is absorbed before the rice is cooked, add a little more and cook until the rice is tender.

In the meantime, make the dressing. Place all the ingredients in a large bowl, whisk together and season with salt and freshly ground black pepper. When the rice is cooked, add it to the dressing ingredients, cover and chill until required.

To assemble the salad, add the cashew nuts, onion, cucumber and chives to the rice, toss well together and transfer to a serving dish.

Stone Fruit and Summer Berry Pudding

This is a variation on classic summer pudding.

SERVES 10

10 slices thin, white sliced bread, crusts removed

8 ripe greengages, washed, cut in half and stoned

4 ripe apricots, washed, cut in half and stoned

225g (8oz/1 cup) strawberries, rinsed and hulled

110g (4oz/½ cup) raspberries, rinsed

225g (8oz/1 cup) blackcurrants, stalks removed

110g (4oz/½ cup) caster sugar

150ml (¼ pint/⅝ cup) crème de cassis or apple juice

4 ripe peaches or nectarines

A few sprigs of red and white currants

A handful of raspberries

1 peach, sliced

Sprigs of mint, to decorate

Cut six slices of bread into rectangular strips to line two 0.75ltr (1½ pint) pudding basins. Cut out a disc from each of the remaining slices to fit the top and bottom of each basin.

Place the greengages and apricots in a large saucepan with the strawberries, raspberries and blackcurrants. Sprinkle the caster sugar and crème de cassis over the top and leave to stand for 15min.

Peel the peaches by plunging them into boiling water for 1min, transferring to a bowl of cold water and peeling away the skin. Cut in half, remove the stone and slice thickly.

Heat the fruit (except the peaches) gently until the sugar has dissolved. Bring to the boil and cook very gently for 5–7min, or until the fruit has softened a little. Strain the fruit into a bowl and reserve the juice.

Dip the bread in the fruit juice until well moistened and use to line the pudding basins.

Mix the peaches with the cooked fruit and divide between the basins. Cover the puddings with the larger rounds of bread, then place a saucer or small plate with a weight on top to press lightly on the puddings. Chill for a minimum of 2 hours.

To serve, turn the puddings out on to a large serving dish and spoon any remaining juice over the top. Use the white and red currants, raspberries, peach and sprigs of mint to decorate.

FATHER'S DAY

Inspired by the modern Mother's Day, Father's Day is now firmly established in its own right and is celebrated on a Sunday, usually in June.

This Sunday family barbecue is to celebrate Father's Day. Choose one or two ideas from the list and serve with green leaf salads or any salad from the book.

FATHER'S DAY BARBECUE

Sticky Barbecue Ribs
Chicken Burgers with Avocado Salsa
Honey and Ginger Summer Vegetable Kebabs
Red Berry Pudding
Cinnamon Meringues
Blackcurrant Parfait

Complete the menu with Wild and Brown Basmati Rice Salad (see page 177) and perhaps a simple green salad, too. A chilled Chilean Chardonnay would suit this alfresco lunch perfectly.

Sticky Barbecue Ribs

These ribs are cooked slowly in the oven and reheated or finished on a hot barbecue.

SERVES 6

| 12 spare ribs |
| 1 tbsp sesame oil |
| 1 tsbp tomato purée |
| 1 tbsp runny honey |
| 110g (4oz/1½ cups) plum jam |
| 3 tbsp soy sauce |
| 4 spring onions, finely chopped |
| 1 clove garlic, crushed |

Put the spare ribs into a large plastic bag. Mix the sesame oil, tomato purée and honey together and season with freshly ground black pepper. Pour the marinade over the ribs and chill for at least 2 hours.

Heat the oven to 170ºC (325ºF/gas mark 3). Arrange the marinated ribs in a roasting tin and pour over the juices from the bag. Cover with aluminium foil and bake for 1 hour, or until tender, basting with the juices during cooking. If the juices begin to burn, add a couple of tablespoons of water during the cooking.

Meanwhile, make the barbecue glaze. Place the plum jam, soy sauce, spring onions and garlic together in a small saucepan, bring to the boil and simmer for 2–3min.

Set the cooked ribs over the hot coals of the barbecue, and cook for 2–3min on each side. Brush generously with glaze and continue to cook for a further 2–3min, or until sticky and brown, but not burnt. Serve very hot.

Chicken Burgers with Avocado Salsa

SERVES 6

2 chicken breasts, skin removed

8 chicken drumsticks, skin removed

1 tbsp chopped rosemary

1 tbsp chopped parsley

1 red onion, finely chopped

2 ripe avocados

Juice of ½ lemon

2 tbsp muscovado or dark brown sugar

2 tbsp chilli dipping sauce

2 ripe beefsteak tomatoes

1 tbsp chopped parsley

1 tsp ground coriander

6 wholemeal baps

Cut the chicken breast into pieces and strip the meat from the chicken drumsticks. Put the meat into a food processor with the herbs and season with salt and black pepper. Whizz together until finely chopped, but not puréed. Add the red onion and pulse on and off a couple of times to mix into the chicken.

Shape the mixture into 6 burgers to fit the baps. Chill the meat for at least 30min, or until you are ready to cook.

Meanwhile, make the salsa. Stone, peel and dice the avocados. Place in a bowl, add the lemon juice, brown sugar and chilli dipping sauce, and mix well.

Deseed and dice the tomatoes. Add to the avocados with the parsley and coriander, and mix well. Season to taste with salt and freshly ground black pepper and chill until required.

Cook the burgers over a hot barbecue for 6–8min on each side, or until the chicken is cooked all the way through. Pierce the middle of each burger to make sure the juices run clear.

Split the baps and grill the cut side on the barbecue for 1–2min. Sandwich the burgers and salsa between the warm baps.

Honey and Ginger Summer Vegetable Kebabs

SERVES 6

1 large aubergine, cut into 2.5cm (1in) chunks

2 courgettes, cut into 2.5cm (1in) chunks

2 carrots, peeled and cut into thick slices

12 small new potatoes, scrubbed

3 small onions, peeled and halved

2 tbsp sunflower oil

A pinch of cayenne pepper

2 tbsp runny honey

5cm (2in) root ginger, peeled and grated

Juice of 1/2 lemon

1 tsp ground cumin

1 tsp poppy seeds

6 skewers

Heat the oven to 180ºC (350ºF/gas mark 4).

Place the vegetables in a large roasting tin, drizzle the oil over the top and season with salt, freshly ground black pepper and cayenne pepper. Toss together and cover with aluminium foil. Bake for 30min, or until just tender.

Mix together the honey, ginger, lemon juice, cumin and poppy seeds, and pour the dressing over the cooked vegetables. Return the roasting tin to the oven for 2min, then remove and leave to cool.

Thread the cold vegetables on to the skewers and baste with any honey dressing left in the tin. Chill and serve.

Red Berry Pudding

SERVES 6

225g (8oz/1 cup) raspberries

225g (8oz/1 cup) strawberries

110g (4oz/½ cup) redcurrants

4 tbsp rosewater

2 tsp caster sugar

4 tbsp crème de cassis (optional)

300ml (½ pint/1¼ cups) Greek yoghurt

300ml (½ pint/1¼ cups) custard

55g (2oz/¼ cup) milk chocolate, grated

Wash all the fruit, hull the strawberries and pull the redcurrants from their stalks with the prongs of a fork. Place in a large glass bowl and add the rosewater, caster sugar and crème de cassis, if using.

Mix the yoghurt and custard together and spoon over the top. Sprinkle the grated chocolate on top and refrigerate for at least 30min.

Cinnamon Meringues

If thoroughly cooked, these meringues will store in an airtight container for several weeks.

MAKES 25–30

3 egg whites

110g (4oz/$\frac{1}{2}$ cup) caster sugar

55g (2oz/$\frac{1}{4}$ cup) soft light brown sugar

2 tsp ground cinnamon

Heat the oven to 100ºC (200ºF/gas mark $\frac{1}{2}$). Line two baking sheets with non-stick baking parchment.

Whisk the egg whites in a clean, dry glass or metal bowl, until very stiff. Add the caster sugar, 1 tbsp at a time, whisking very well between each addition, until the meringue becomes very glossy and will form stiff peaks – don't add the sugar too quickly, or it will become soft.

Sift the brown sugar and cinnamon together, sprinkle over the meringue mixture and quickly fold together until the sugar is just incorporated, but the meringue peaks remain stiff.

Spoon or pipe rounds on to the lined baking sheets and bake on the bottom shelf of the oven for 1 hour. Remove and tap a hole in the base of each meringue, then turn each on its side and bake for a further 30min. Leave to cool on a wire rack.

Serve with the Red Berry Pudding (see page 183) or alone, sandwiched with some whipped cream lightly sweetened with sugar.

Blackcurrant Parfait

Make this dessert a day in advance, if possible, or at least 6 hours ahead.

SERVES 6

450g (1lb/2 cups) blackcurrants

110g (4oz/$^1/_2$ cup) caster sugar

150ml ($^1/_4$ pint/$^5/_8$ cup) blackcurrant cordial

3 egg whites

300ml ($^1/_2$ pint/1$^1/_4$ cups) whipping cream

Icing sugar, to serve

Pull the blackcurrants from their stalks with the prongs of a fork and rinse thoroughly. Place the currants in a saucepan with 2 tbsp of the sugar and the blackcurrant cordial. Bring to the boil, reduce the heat and simmer for 5min, or until the fruit skins have popped. Remove from the heat and rub the blackcurrants through a sieve to remove the seeds. Leave for 30min to cool completely.

Whisk the egg whites in a clean, dry glass or metal bowl until very stiff. Add the remaining caster sugar, 1 tbsp at a time, whisking very well between each addition until the meringue is glossy and forms stiff peaks.

Whip the cream until soft peaks form and fold into the meringue with the blackcurrant purée. Add a little icing sugar if necessary, to taste.

Spoon the parfait mixture into a freezer-proof container and freeze for at least 6 hours, and preferably overnight.

Remove from the freezer and leave to soften in the refrigerator for 30min before serving.

SUMMER HARVEST

Like autumn, summer brings an abundance of fruits and vegetables to be stored for enjoyment later on in the year.

Harvest festival is traditionally celebrated in autumn, but it can be celebrated during the summer months too. Just remember when you are making jams or jellies to choose the best quality fruit that is only just ripe and not damaged in any way.

SUMMER HARVEST PPRESERVES

Mixed Currant Jelly
Raspberry and Greengage Liqueur Conserve
Old-fashioned Strawberry Jam
Beetroot, Shallot and Raisin Chutney

Mixed Currant Jelly

This jelly can be stored in a cool dark place for several months.

MAKES 2KG (4.4LB)

1kg (2.2lb/5 cups) blackcurrants

1kg (2.2lb/5 cups) redcurrants

1ltr (1^3/$_4$ pint/4^1/$_2$ cups) water

Preserving sugar, warmed

Jam jars and covers

Wash the fruit and place in a large saucepan or preserving pan with the water, bring to the boil and cook over a low heat for 20–25min or until the fruit is soft and beginning to break up.

Pour the fruit and juice into a jelly cloth, set over a large bowl, and leave to drip for 2–3 hours.

To sterilize the jam jars, heat the oven to 100ºC (200ºF/gas mark ^{1}/$_2$). Wash jars in hot soapy water and put to dry, upside down on a baking sheet, in the oven.

When the fruit is drained, discard it (or reserve it for other recipes) and measure the juice. To every 600ml (1pint/2^1/$_2$ cups), add 450g (1lb/2 cups) preserving sugar. Replace the juice in the preserving pan, add the measured sugar and heat gently until the sugar has dissolved. Bring to the boil and simmer for 12–15min, or until the jelly reaches setting point. To test for this, put a small spoonful of jelly on to a saucer and chill for 5min – it's done if a thick skin forms and wrinkles when you push a spoon through it

If the jam is ready, remove it from the heat and skim off any white residue on the surface. Transfer to a jug and divide between the jam jars. Cover each with a wax disc and cellophane secured with an elastic band. Label the jars when cold.

Greengage and Raspberry Liqueur Conserve

The jam will store in a cool dark place for several months.

MAKES 2KG (4.4LB)

1kg (2.2lb/5 cups) greengages, washed, stoned and diced

600ml (1 pint/2¹/2 cups) water

1kg (2.2lb/ 5 cups) raspberries

1.8kg (4lb/8 cups) preserving sugar

300ml (¹/2 pint/1¹/2 cups) crème de framboise

Jam jars and covers

Place the greengages and water in a large saucepan or preserving pan. Bring to the boil and simmer for 5min. Add the raspberries and sugar and heat gently until the sugar has dissolved.

Bring the fruit back to the boil, then lower the heat and simmer for 12–15min, then add the crème de framboise and simmer for a further 5min, or until the conserve reaches setting point. To test for this, put a small spoonful of jelly on to a saucer and chill for 5min – it's done if a thick skin forms and wrinkles when you push a spoon through it.

When the conserve is ready, remove the pan from the heat and skim away any white residue. Leave to stand for 30min.

Meanwhile, sterilize the jam jars. Heat the oven to 100°C (200°F/gas mark ¹/2). Wash jars in hot soapy water and put to dry, upside down on a baking sheet, in the oven.

Transfer the cooled conserve to a jug and divide between the jam jars. Cover each with a wax disc and cellophane secured with an elastic band. Label the jars when cold.

Old-fashioned Strawberry Jam

Strawberries have a low pectin content and therefore need added acidity to help the jam to set. I've chosen to use lemon juice, but using other fruit such as gooseberries or rhubarb would be a good substitute.

MAKES 1.3KG (3LB)

1kg (2.2lb/5 cups) small strawberries, hulled and washed

1kg (2.2lb/8 cups) preserving sugar

Juice and grated zest of 3 lemons

Jam jars and covers

Put the prepared strawberries into a large bowl and stir in the sugar. Cover and leave to stand for at least 2 hours.

Transfer the strawberries and sugar to a preserving pan and add the lemon zest and juice. Bring to the boil, lower the heat and simmer for 20–25min, or until setting point is reached. To test for this, put a small spoonful of jam on to a saucer and chill for 5min – it's done if a thick skin forms and wrinkles when you push a spoon through it.

Remove from the heat and skim off any white residue. Leave to stand for at least 30min.

Meanwhile, sterilize the jam jars. Heat the oven to 100°C (200°F/gas mark ½). Wash the jars in hot soapy water and put to dry, upside down on a baking sheet, in the oven. Transfer the cooled jam to a jug and divide between the jars. Cover each with a wax disc and cellophane secured with an elastic band. Label the jars when cold.

Beetroot, Shallot and Raisin Chutney

This chutney can be stored for 1 month in a cool place before eating.

MAKES 3KG (7LB)

1kg (2.2lb) beetroot, unpeeled

1kg (2.2lb) shallots, peeled
and halved

2 cloves garlic, finely chopped

225g (8oz/1¼ cups) raisins

1 tbsp salt

1kg (2.2lb/5⅞ cups) soft dark
brown sugar

1.1ltr (2 pints/5 cups) malt
vinegar

Cook the beetroot in boiling water for 50min, or until the skin becomes loose and will peel away. Peel and cut into chunks.

Place the beetroot, along with all the remaining ingredients, in a large saucepan or preserving pan and bring to the boil. Lower the heat and simmer for 1½–2 hours, or until the vegetables are soft and the chutney has a thick pulpy consistency.

Remove from the heat and leave to cool for 30min.

Meanwhile, sterilize the jam jars. Heat the oven to 100°C (200°F/gas mark ½). Wash the jars in hot soapy water and put to dry, upside down on a baking sheet, in the oven.

Transfer the cooled chutney to a jug and divide between the jars. Cover each with a wax disc and cellophane secured with an elastic band. Label the jars when cold.

Autumn Feasts

With the drawing in of the days and the end of summer, officially on 8 September, autumn is traditionally a time for harvesting and thankfulness for the opportunities of the warmer months. Festivals to celebrate the year's bounty have been taking place throughout the world for thousands of years. Every religion or creed has its own festivities for the provision of food.

Autumn is also a rather sad time, bringing the knowledge that colder months are around the corner. The autumn equinox, when the hours of daylight and dark are equal, occurs on 23 September. Yet in nature it is a beautiful time of year – the leaves on the trees turn to reds, golds and yellows, the mornings are misty and the autumn sun is still warming, although less bright.

Several important Jewish festivals take place in the autumn months. The Jewish New Year, Rosh Hashanah, occurs towards the end of September or the beginning of October. It is celebrated over two days and is both solemn and hopeful. Honey is a symbolic food for the Jewish New Year; apples dipped in honey are eaten and prayers are said, asking God for a sweet year. Recipes for this special occasion are legion –

pulses, various types of bread and foods mentioned in the Torah, particularly the pomegranate, are all included in the celebrations. The Jewish nation is so widespread that ingredients and therefore prepared dishes vary widely from one continent to another, but their symbolism remains constant.

Yom Kippur, the Day of Atonement, is celebrated ten days after Rosh Hashanah. It is a day of fasting and prayer, an opportunity to make amends for wrongdoing and to give to the poor. The meal on the afternoon of Yom Kippur eve is traditionally very simple and quite bland. Spicy or particularly salty food is not served at this occasion.

Sukkoth, the Feast of Tabernacles, follows shortly after Yom Kippur. This feast lasts for eight days and commemorates the time the Jews spent in the wilderness. The Sukkoth itself is a tent-like dwelling erected during the festival. Made of temporary materials, as the dwellings of the Jews would have been, it symbolizes God's protection.

For the Christian Church there are important saints' days during the autumn months. Mary, Christ's mother, is held in high esteem and is considered the greatest saint within the Catholic Church. There are three main feast days celebrating her role in the life of Christ and her personal attribute of faith. One in particular, her nativity feast day, is on 8 September, a very important day for the Catholic faith.

The feast of St Michael (the archangel) and All Angels is celebrated on 29 September. Michaelmas or the Mass of St Michael, as it was known, has almost been forgotten today, although, it was at one time of great spiritual and agricultural importance. So was the feast of St Martin, more commonly known as Martinmas, which takes place on 11 November. Its date coincided with the beginning of the old Celtic winter and was the time when any excessive livestock were slaughtered. It was, too, a time to plan for winter and the cold months ahead. A spell of fine weather in November is often called St Martin's Summer. The feast of St Andrew, the patron saint of Scotland (and incidentally of Russia), takes place on 30 November. Andrew was a fisherman who became one of Christ's apostles.

At the end of October and the beginning of November the Church celebrates three festival days to remember all those, both saints and ordinary people, who have gone before us. All Hallows' Eve, or Halloween, is on the last day of October: the two following days, 1 and 2 November, are All Saints' Day and All Souls' Day. It is around this time that the church calendar draws to a close and a new year begins, looking forward again to the cycle of Christmas and the birth of Jesus.

In Britain 5 November is the celebration of the capture of the legendary folk hero Guy Fawkes, and the foiling of his attempt to blow up the Houses of Parliament. It is a modern festivity, but one that is celebrated around a bonfire and in much the same way as Halloween.

Thanksgiving, the final feast in this book, focuses on the past, the present and hope for the future. The Pilgrim Fathers celebrated the first Thanksgiving Day at the end of their first year in the New World of North America. With the help of the native Indians, they had established indigenous crops and had reaped a successful harvest. This is the culminating feast in the book and a celebration of everything that we have to be thankful for.

SEASONAL INGREDIENTS IN AUTUMN

While we celebrate the bringing in of the harvest, there are many foods that are bountiful at this time of the year.

The orchard fruits season is well under way by September. Thousands of varieties of apples and pears are harvested worldwide. Many store well and are put aside for the coming months.

Less common are quinces and medlars, not grown commercially in the UK, but still available across Europe. The quince harvest is particularly important in Spain and Portugal, where it is used to make the traditional dish, *membrillo*, a quince paste.

Plums and damsons are also a good buy at this time of the year. The abundance of the crop makes them perfect for jam making and they also freeze very well. Raspberries have their main season earlier in the summer, but good Scottish varieties are in season during September and October.

The summer vegetables, beans, peas and sweetcorn, continue well into October, when the roots and tubers begin to take over. By

October we have a good supply of celeriac and swedes.

The brassica group of vegetables, including broccoli, calabrese, cauliflower and cabbage, keep going. Essential for Christmas, Brussels sprouts come into season in November and are a good, filling and inexpensive vegetable.

Tomatoes are still available through the autumn months, but it is really the time for marrows, pumpkins and winter squashes; these, unlike the summer courgette, have a thick skin that needs to be peeled and pithy seeds that do not soften on cooking.

Once the frosts have come many of the more delicate summer plants begin to die off. Herbs are no exception. By November, unless there has been no frost, only the hearty herbs are growing: rosemary, sage and thyme.

Although we concentrate on commercial farming and growing, plenty of foods still grow wild in the hedgerows and woods. In the summer months elderflowers give off a heady fragrance; left to their own devices, heavily laden heads of elderberries ripen in September and these can be used in jellies, jams, pies and crumbles or in making elderberry wine. The hedgerows also bring quantities of blackberries, or brambles, in August and September. The old wives' law that blackberries should not be picked in October, lest the devil has spat on them, is probably to do with the fact that once a frost has come the fruit taste bitter and are likely to contain maggots.

Sloes, the wild member of the plum family, are also found in October. Unlike blackberries, they are usually best left until there has been a frost; extremely tart at the best of times, the frost mellows their flavour somewhat and they make good jelly.

Rose hips and haws packed full of vitamin C make the hedgerow a colourful sight. They are hard and pithy, but make a great addition to jellies, jams or syrup for the inevitable winter coughs and colds.

Wild mushrooms are also around from September. They are available in the supermarket, but are very expensive; it is, however, inadvisable to try and collect your own unless you know exactly what to look for. The earthy, rich flavours of these add a fantastic twist to many rich casseroles.

Sweet chestnuts are also collectable come October, although the very best cultivated variety come from France later in the year. Washed, pierced and roasted in a fire, they are delicious and low in fat, although messy to eat.

The expression 'Each to his season' is an opportunity to reflect on our own life and mortality, but also on the seasons of the year and what each season chooses to bring to us. So after a long year we have many things to celebrate and enjoy.

Harvest Festival Bread

It seems fitting to have a savoury bread to celebrate autumn after the harvest of cereal crops. It's not a true bread and needs no 'proving', so it's very easy to make.

---

2 tbsp extra virgin olive oil

140g (5oz/1cup) butternut squash, peeled and diced

1 courgette, thinly sliced

450g (1lb/3^1/2 cups) plain flour

2 tsp salt

2 tsp bicarbonate of soda

4 tsp cream of tartar

225g (8oz/1^3/4 cups) wholemeal flour

600 ml (1 pint/2^3/4 cups) buttermilk

5 tbsp pesto

30g (1oz/^{1}/4 cup) pumpkin or sunflower seeds

5 tbsp sundried tomato paste

12 black or green olives (optional)

85g (3oz/^{1}/2 cup) feta cheese, diced

1 tsp fresh thyme, chopped

1 clove garlic, chopped

30g (1oz/^{1}/4 cup) pine nuts

30g (1oz/^{1}/2 cup) freshly grated Parmesan cheese

Heat the olive oil in a frying pan and sauté the butternut squash for 4–5min in the olive oil, add the courgette and cook for a further 5min. Season to taste with salt and black pepper.

Heat the oven to 190ºC (375ºF/gas mark 5). Lightly dust a large baking sheet with flour.

Sift the plain flour, salt, bicarbonate of soda and cream of tartar together. Divide the sifted flour between two large bowls and add half the wholemeal flour to each bowl.

Divide the buttermilk between two more bowls. Add the pesto and pumpkin seeds to one and the sundried tomato paste and olives to the other, and mix both well.

Pour the pesto buttermilk mix into one bowl of flour and stir to form a soft, but not sticky, dough. Add the tomato buttermilk mix to the other bowl of flour and stir to form a similar dough.

Turn both doughs on to a floured board and knead very lightly. Roll each into a round about 23cm (9in) in diameter. Place the pesto dough on the baking sheet and sprinkle the feta cheese, thyme and garlic over the top. Place the sundried tomato dough on top and press the two together lightly, then make a slight indentation on the top.

Bake for 20min on the top shelf of the oven, then reduce the temperature to 170ºC (325ºF/gas mark 3) and bake for a further 10min. Remove from the oven and spoon the butternut squash and courgette mixture on top. Sprinkle cheese and pine nuts over the bread and return it to the oven for a further 30min, or until the bread is cooked and the cheese is golden brown.

Transfer to a wire rack to cool, then cut into wedges and serve.

AUTUMN SUNDAY FAMILY LUNCH

For us Sundays have changed so much over the last few years. Many shops remain open all week and there are very few things that you can't buy or access, so the day of rest is beginning to fade away and the weeks seem to roll into one. These opportunities are great, but with no break from the relentless activity of day-to-day life during the week, there seems to be little rest.

Sunday is a special day. Not only is it the beginning of a new week, but it has been designated as a day of rest for centuries, right back to the beginning of the Bible. A day of rest in some cultures means just that – no work of any kind and a time for spiritual reflection.

So Sundays are a good day to break with the routine of the week, to get together with friends and family and enjoy a meal.

AUTUMN SUNDAY LUNCH

Lamb, Tomato and Barley Hot Pot
Poppy Seed Honey Carrots
Steamed Blackberry and Apple Pudding
Cinnamon Walnut Cream

To complete the menu, serve the hot pot with marrow, courgettes or broccoli. Accompany the meal with an Australian Cabernet Sauvignon.

Lamb, Tomato and Barley Hot Pot

SERVES 4

675g (1¹/₂lb) of lamb neck fillets

2 tbsp plain flour

A large pinch of cayenne pepper

¹/₂ tsp ground allspice

2 tbsp sunflower oil

15g (¹/₂oz/¹/₂ tbsp) butter

2 large onions, each cut into
8 wedges

1 clove garlic, crushed

4 tbsp pearl barley

1 tbsp tomato purée

1 tbsp soft dark brown sugar

400g (14oz/2 cups) tinned
tomatoes

600ml (1 pint/2¹/₂ cups) beef stock

1 bay leaf

4 sprigs of rosemary

1 tbsp chopped parsley

Heat the oven to 160ºC (300ºF/gas mark 2).

Trim the lamb fillets, removing any sinews or membrane, and cut each into 2 or 3 thick slices.

Mix the flour, cayenne and allspice together and season with salt and black pepper.

Toss the lamb pieces in the flour and shake off any excess.

Heat the oil and butter together in a large casserole pot and sear a few pieces of lamb at a time. Set the meat aside.

Reduce the heat and add the onion to the pot. Cook until soft, then add the garlic, pearl barley, tomato purée and brown sugar and cook for 1–2min.

Add the tomatoes and beef stock to the pot, bring to the boil and add the herbs. Replace the lamb and season lightly with salt and black pepper. Cover the pot and cook for 1¹/₂–2 hours, or until the lamb and pearl barley are tender.

Remove the lamb from the pot and set aside. Skim off any excess fat from the cooking liquid, then reduce it to about 300ml (¹/₂ pint/1¹/₄ cups) by boiling it rapidly. Adjust the seasoning and discard the bay leaf and rosemary. Return the meat to the pot, stir in the parsley and serve hot.

Poppy Seed and Honey Carrots

SERVES 4

450g (1lb) carrots, peeled
and thickly sliced

1 tbsp runny honey

1 tbsp sesame oil

1 tbsp poppy seeds

Put the carrots into a large saucepan and add enough water to just cover them. Add the honey and sesame oil, and season with a little salt and freshly ground black pepper.

Cover the saucepan, bring to the boil and simmer until the carrots are nearly tender. Remove the lid and boil very rapidly to allow the water to evaporate, taking care that the carrots don't burn.

Once the water has gone, add the poppy seeds and toss the carrots to coat them thoroughly. Serve very hot.

Steamed Blackberry and Apple Pudding

SERVES 4

4 tbsp blackberry jelly or blackcurrant jam

110g (4oz/^{1}/2 cup) blackberries

1 small Bramley cooking apple, peeled and diced

1 tbsp soft light brown sugar

170g (6oz/^{3}/4 cup) unsalted butter or margarine

170g (6oz/^{3}/4 cup) caster sugar

3 eggs, beaten

170g (6oz/1 cup and 2 tbsp) self-raising flour, sifted

1 tsp ground cinnamon

1–2 tbsp milk

Spread the jam across the base of a 1ltr (1^3/4 pint/4^1/2 cup) buttered pudding basin.

Mix the blackberries, apple and brown sugar together and add to the pudding basin.

Cream the butter and caster sugar together until light, fluffy and very pale. Add the beaten eggs, a splash at a time, beating well between each addition.

Once all the eggs have been incorporated, fold in the flour, cinnamon and milk until the mixture has a soft dropping consistency. Spoon the mixture on top of the fruit – the basin should be about two-thirds full.

Cover the basin with a double sheet of non-stick baking parchment, topped with aluminium foil. Secure very carefully with string and trim the excess paper and foil.

Carefully lower the pudding basin into a large saucepan of enough boiling water to come two-thirds of the way up the basin. Cover the saucepan and steam the pudding for 1^1/2 hours, keeping the water level topped up with boiling water.

After this time, remove the foil and paper to check the pudding – it should be firm, springy to the touch and beginning to shrink from the sides of the basin. If it needs further cooking, replace the cover, retie the string and steam for a further 15min before rechecking.

When cooked, turn the pudding on to a serving plate and keep it warm in a low oven. Serve with the Cinnamon Walnut Cream.

Cinnamon Walnut Cream

SERVES 4

30g (1oz/$\frac{1}{8}$ cup) butter

2 tbsp caster sugar

1 tsp ground cinnamon

55g (2oz/$\frac{1}{2}$ cup) chopped walnuts

150ml ($\frac{1}{4}$ pint/$1\frac{1}{4}$ cups) natural yoghurt

150ml ($\frac{1}{4}$ pint/$1\frac{1}{4}$ cups) custard

Melt the butter in a saucepan and add the sugar, cinnamon and walnuts. Cook over a medium heat for 2–3min, or until the sugar is lightly caramelized, but not burnt. Pour into a bowl and leave to cool.

Mix the yoghurt and custard together, then stir it into the walnut mixture and serve immediately.

AUTUMN HARVEST

The autumn harvest was and still is a time of thanksgiving and celebration for all cultures in every country around the globe. Basic survival depends on a good harvest and it is appropriate to be thankful, although in a busy world it is easy to forget how much we have.

Our Harvest thanksgiving begins with a selection of preserves which make the most of produce that is only in season for a short while, particularly that which grows wild in the hedgerows. To follow we have a Harvest Festival supper – a celebration that takes place in many churches across the country.

AUTUMN HARVEST PRESERVES

Boxing Day Rescue Chutney
Autumn Greenhouse Pickle
Old-fashioned Blackberry Vinegar
Apple and Bay Jelly
Aromatic Plum, Damson and Sloe Cheese
Spicy Pickled Onions

SERVES 10

Field Mushroom Gratin
Chicken and Ratatouille Pasta Pie
Mulled Quinces

If you are cooking an informal supper for a larger number this menu can be prepared well in advance. To accompany the meal you will need some bread; a baguette or something crusty is ideal. A colourful vegetable dish or salad is perfect with the chicken dish – just make sure you have lots of crisp textures.

To complete the menu, serve the quinces with Treacle Snaps (see page 150). Serve an Australian Pinot Noir with this supper.

Old-fashioned Blackberry Vinegar

This recipe works equally well with mulberries or raspberries. The vinegar is prepared over a period of four days.

1kg (2.2lb/4^1/2 cups) fresh blackberries

225g (8oz/1 cup) caster sugar

1ltr (1^3/4 pints/4^1/2 cups) white wine vinegar

A selection of bottles with tops

Place half of the blackberries in a large bowl with the sugar and vinegar, stir well, cover and keep in a cool place for 1 day.

The next day, strain the vinegar and pour it into a clean bowl. Add the remaining blackberries, cover and leave in a cool place for 2 days.

Meanwhile, sterilize the bottles. Heat the oven to 100°C (200°F/gas mark ^{1}/2). Wash the bottles in hot soapy water and put to dry, upside down on a baking sheet, in the oven.

Strain the vinegar once more and pour into the sterilized bottles. Seal and refrigerate for at least 14 days before use.

Autumn Greenhouse Pickle

MAKES 2KG (4.4LB)

450g (1lb) ripe tomatoes, peeled and diced

450g (1lb) green tomatoes, peeled and diced

1 aubergine, diced

1 cucumber, diced

1 large onion, roughly chopped

2 red chillis, finely chopped

3 red peppers, diced

3 tbsp salt (preferably coarse sea salt)

225g (8oz/1 1/3 cups) soft dark brown sugar

2 tsp mustard seeds

1 tsp ground allspice

400ml (3/4 pint/1 1/4 cups) malt vinegar

2 tbsp whole pickling spices

Jam jars and covers

Place the prepared vegetables in a large bowl, add the salt and mix well. Cover and leave to stand for a minimum of 6 hours, and preferably overnight.

The next day, drain away any liquid and pat vegetables dry with absorbent kitchen paper.

Transfer the vegetables to a large saucepan or preserving pan and add the sugar, mustard seeds and allspice. Leave to stand for 30min.

Meanwhile, sterilize the jam jars. Heat the oven to 100ºC (200ºF/gas mark 1/2). Wash jars in hot soapy water and put to dry, upside down on a baking sheet, in the oven.

Pour the vinegar and pickling spices into a saucepan, bring to the boil, remove from the heat and leave to infuse for 10min.

Strain the vinegar over the vegetables and bring the mixture to the boil. Simmer over a low heat for 40–50min, or until the vegetables are tender and the mixture quite stiff, but still moist. Remove from the heat and leave to stand for 10min.

Transfer the pickle to a jug, then fill the sterilized jars. Cover each with a wax disc and cellophane secured with an elastic band. Label the jars when cold and store for a few weeks before serving.

Boxing Day Rescue Chutney

This chutney will be ready to enjoy with cold meats such as turkey and ham left over after the Christmas feast.

MAKES 2KG (4.4LB)

1kg (2.2lb) ripe Conference dessert pears, peeled, cores removed and diced

1kg (2.2lb) Bramley cooking apples, peeled, cores removed and diced

225g (8oz/1 cup) dried cranberries

225g (8oz/1 cup) semi-dried figs, chopped

1 large onion, peeled and chopped

1 tsp cayenne pepper

2 tsp curry powder

5cm (2in) piece of root ginger, peeled and grated

2 cloves garlic, chopped

1 tsp ground cloves

1 tbsp salt

450g (1lb/2½ cups) soft light brown sugar

600ml (1 pint/2½ cups) white malt vinegar

Jam jars and covers

Put all the ingredients into a large saucepan or preserving pan and stir well. Bring to the boil and then reduce to simmering point. Cook the mixture for 2–2½ hours, or until very thick.

Meanwhile, sterilize the jam jars. Heat the oven to 100°C (200°F/gas mark ½). Wash jars in hot soapy water and put to dry, upside down on a baking sheet, in the oven.

When the chutney is ready, remove from the heat and leave to cool for 15min. Ladle the mixture into the prepared jars and cover each with a wax disc and cellophane secured with an elastic band. Label the jars when cold. Store in a cool dark place for a minimum of 2 weeks before serving.

Apple and Bay Jelly

2kg (4.4lb) cooking apples, washed and chopped roughly

1ltr (1³/4 pints/4¹/2 cups) water

8 bay leaves

2 sticks cinnamon

300ml (¹/2 pint/1¹/4 cups) cider vinegar

Preserving sugar, warmed

Jam jars and covers

Place the apples, water, 4 bay leaves and the cinnamon in a large saucepan and mix well. Bring to the boil, then reduce the heat and simmer for 25–30min, or until the apples are soft.

Add the vinegar, bring to the boil and simmer for 5min.

Pour the apples and liquids into a jelly bag or piece of muslin set over a large bowl. Leave to strain for at least 4 hours.

Meanwhile, sterilize the jam jars. Heat the oven to 100°C (200°F/gas mark ¹/2). Wash the jars in hot soapy water and put to dry, upside down on a baking sheet, in the oven.

When the fruit is fully strained, discard the apple pulp. Measure the liquid strained off and for every 600ml (1 pint/2¹/2 cups), add 450g (1lb/2 cups) warm preserving sugar. Heat the liquid in a saucepan over a low flame until the sugar is dissolved. Bring to the boil, add the remaining bay leaves and simmer until setting point is reached. To test for this, put a small spoonful of jelly on to a saucer and chill for 5min – it's done if a thick skin forms and wrinkles when you push a spoon through it.

When setting point is reached, remove the jelly from the heat and transfer to a clean jug. Fill the prepared jars, cover each with a wax disc and cellophane secured with an elastic band. Label the jars when cold and store in a cool dark place for at least 2 weeks before use.

Aromatic Plum, Damson and Sloe Cheese

A fruit cheese is a thick, sweetened fruit pulp. If damsons and sloes are unavailable, use more plums in their place.

1kg (2.2lb) plums, stoned and diced

225g (8oz) damsons

225g (8oz) sloes

8 star anise

1 stick of cinnamon

4 sprigs of sage

4 sprigs of thyme

5cm (2in) piece of root ginger, peeled and chopped

300ml (^{1}/2 pint/1^1/4 cups) dry red wine

150ml (^{1}/4 pint/ ^{5}/8 cup) water

Preserving sugar

A large jar

Place the plums, damsons and sloes in a large saucepan, add the spices, herbs, ginger and red wine and simmer over a low heat until the fruit is very hot.

Remove from the heat and rub the fruit through a sieve, discarding any remaining skin or stones.

Measure the strained pulp, return it to the saucepan and for every 600ml (1pint/2^1/2 cups) pulp, add 560g (1^1/4lb/2^1/2 cups) preserving sugar. Cook over a very low heat, stirring every so often to prevent the mixture from sticking, for 20–25min, or until the mixture is very thick and sticky. Leave to cool.

Meanwhile, sterilize the jam jars. Heat the oven to 100°C (200°F/gas mark ^{1}/2). Wash jars in hot soapy water and put to dry, upside down on a baking sheet, in the oven.

Pour the jelly into the sterilized jars and cover with a wax disc and cellophane secured with an elastic band. Label and store in a cool place for 1 month before use.

Spicy Pickled Onions

These are prepared 36 hours before pickling.

MAKES 1KG (2.2LB)

1.35kg (3lb) pickling onions, peeled

170g (6oz/⅔ cup) coarse sea salt

750ml–1ltr (1½–1¾ pints/3–4½ cups) spiced vinegar

1 tbsp dried chilli flakes

1 tbsp mustard seeds

2 cinnamon sticks

2 bay leaves

Screw-top jars

Place the pickling onions in a large bowl, sprinkle the salt over them, cover and leave to stand in a cool place for 36 hours.

The next day, place the vinegar, chilli flakes, mustard seeds, cinnamon sticks and bay leaves in a saucepan and bring to the boil. Remove from the heat and leave to infuse for 1 hour, or until cool.

Meanwhile, sterilize the jars. Heat the oven to 100°C (200°F/gas mark ½). Wash jars in hot soapy water and put to dry, upside down on a baking sheet, in the oven.

Drain the onions and pat dry with absorbent kitchen paper. Pack the onions into the sterilized jars and pour the pickled vinegar over the top, to completely cover the onions. Cover the jars and store in a cool place for 3 weeks before use.

Field Mushroom Gratin

SERVES 10

20 cup mushrooms approximately 7.5cm (3in) in diameter

340g (12oz/4 cups) mixed mushrooms, such as shiitake, oyster and button

30g (1oz/¼ cup) dried porcini, soaked in 4 tbsp boiling water and drained

2 cloves garlic

8 anchovies (optional) chopped

250g (9oz/1½ cups) cream cheese

3 tbsp chopped parsley

3 tbsp olive oil

6–8 tbsp fresh breadcrumbs

4 tbsp freshly grated Parmesan cheese

Mixed salad leaves, to serve

Heat the oven to 190ºC (375ºF/gas mark 5).

Peel the cup mushrooms and set aside. Put the peelings, mixed mushrooms, porcini, garlic and anchovies into a food processor. Whizz together until chopped finely. Transfer to a bowl and stir in the cream cheese and parsley.

Brush the cup mushrooms with olive oil and season with plenty of freshly ground black pepper. Spoon the cream cheese mixture into the centre of the cup mushrooms. Arrange in an ovenproof dish and sprinkle the breadcrumbs and cheese over the top.

Bake the mushrooms for 20min, or until the mushrooms are piping hot and the gratin crusts are brown. Arrange on the salad leaves and serve.

Chicken and Ratatouille Pasta Pie

SERVES 10

6 tbsp olive oil

1 red chilli, chopped

2 tsp ground coriander

2 large aubergines, diced

2 onions, finely sliced

2 cloves garlic, crushed

2 x 400g (14oz/4 cups) tinned tomatoes

4 courgettes, diced

2 tbsp tomato purée

6 chicken breasts, skinned and diced

2 tbsp dark brown sugar

3 tbsp Worcestershire sauce

900g (2lb/10 cups) dried tri-coloured pasta shells

300ml ($^{1}/_{2}$ pint/$1^{1}/_{4}$ cups) Greek yoghurt

3 tbsp fresh, chopped herbs, such as parsley, chives, rosemary, thyme

4–5 tbsp freshly grated Parmesan cheese

Heat 3 tbsp of oil in a large saucepan, add the chilli, ground coriander, aubergines and onions and stir-fry over a low heat for 6–7min.

Add the garlic, tomatoes, courgettes and tomato purée, bring to the boil and simmer for 10–12min, or until the vegetables are tender.

Heat the remaining oil in a separate frying pan and stir-fry the chicken until golden brown and just cooked, then add to the tomato mixture, along with the sugar and Worcestershire sauce. Season to taste with salt and black pepper.

Cook the pasta in plenty of boiling water for 10–12min, or until al dente. Drain well and stir two-thirds of the pasta into the chicken and ratatouille mixture. Spoon into a large gratin dish.

Mix the remaining pasta with the yoghurt, herbs and two-thirds of the cheese, and season to taste with salt and black pepper. Spoon the pasta over the chicken mixture and sprinkle the remaining cheese on top.

Bake for 30–40min, or until piping hot and serve immediately.

Mulled Quinces

If quinces are hard to find, use Williams pears for this recipe instead. Serve these with some crisp biscuits – Treacle Snaps (see page 150) are perfect.

SERVES 10

2kg (4.4lb) quinces, peeled, cut into quarters and cores removed

1ltr (1³/4 pints/4¹/2 cups) dry red wine

1ltr (1³/4 pints/4¹/2 cups) water

340g (12oz/1¹/2 cups) granulated sugar

6 clementines or satsumas, peeled and thickly sliced

3 lemons, peeled and thickly sliced

7.5cm (3in) piece root ginger, peeled and chopped

4 cinnamon sticks

8 whole cloves

3 sachets of mulled wine spices

5 tbsp chopped pistachio nuts

1ltr (1¹/2 pints/4 cups) single cream or natural yoghurt, to serve

Heat the oven to 150ºC (300ºF/gas mark 2).

Place the prepared quinces in a large casserole pot with the wine, water and sugar. Bring to the boil over a low heat, stirring occasionally.

Add the clementine and lemon slices, ginger and spices and bring back to the boil. Cover the casserole pot and poach in the oven for 2 hours.

Once the quinces are tender, transfer all the fruit to a large serving dish. Reduce the remaining cooking liquid to 600ml (1 pint) by boiling it rapidly, then add a little more sugar, if necessary, to taste. Pour the syrup over the fruit and sprinkle the pistachio nuts over the top. Serve hot or cold with the cream or yoghurt and Treacle Snaps.

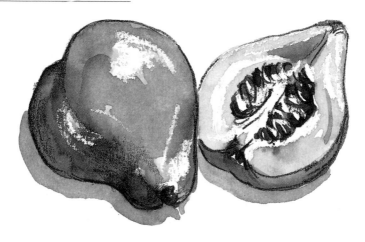

MICHAELMAS

Michaelmas, or the feast day of St Michael and All Angels, takes place on 29 September. Little celebrated today, it was in years past one of the major saints' days around which life revolved. Michaelmas was often the day of the large 'hiring fairs' in Britain. It was an opportunity to employ labourers or household servants.

History relates that geese, fattened during the summer months, were driven, sometimes over long distances, to the nearest fair. To keep the webbed feet of the geese from becoming damaged during the walk, they would often be dipped in tar. Some geese were roasted to celebrate Michaelmas. Others were fattened over the autumn months in time for a traditional Christmas meal.

The market for goose today is mainly over the Christmas period, although it is possible to find them at this time of year. A young bird that has been taken through only to September is often referred to as a green goose. These have less fat than geese sold in midwinter and can dry out easily if not cooked with care.

MICHAELMAS DINNER

SERVES 8

Bacon, Savoy Cabbage and Parsnip Frittata
Roast Goose with Scrumpy and Sage
Baked Pumpkin
Celeriac Fritters
Victoria Plum Clafoutis

To complete the menu, serve the goose with steamed courgettes. Serve a claret with this dinner.

Bacon, Savoy Cabbage and Parsnip Frittata

You will need a very large frying pan to cook this frittata, or cook it in two parts.

SERVES 8

110g (4oz/1 cup) streaky bacon, rind removed, diced

1 onion, finely chopped

^{1}/2 a small Savoy cabbage, finely shredded

3 parsnips, peeled and finely sliced

45g (1^1/2oz/^{1}/6 cup) butter

8 eggs, beaten

150ml (^{1}/4 pint/^{5}/8 cup) double cream

1 tsp grated nutmeg

55g (2oz/^{1}/2 cup) mature Cheddar cheese, grated

A few salad leaves dressed with oil and vinegar, to serve

Cook the bacon in a large frying pan over a low to medium heat until crisp and brown. Transfer it to a plate, leaving as much bacon fat as possible in the pan.

Add the onion to the frying pan and sauté for 8–10min, or until soft, then transfer to a bowl to cool.

Blanch the shredded cabbage in boiling, salted water for 2–3min, drain and briefly rinse under cold running water to stop any further cooking. Drain and pat dry with absorbent kitchen paper.

Cook the parsnip slices in boiling, salted water for 2–3min, or until tender, then drain and dry on absorbent kitchen paper.

Heat the butter in the frying pan until it's nut brown. Heat the grill to its highest setting.

Mix the onion, cabbage, parsnip, eggs and double cream together and season with salt and black pepper and the nutmeg.

Pour the mixture into the frying pan, reduce the heat and cook very gently for 12–15min, or until the egg is nearly set.

Sprinkle the grated cheese over the top of the frittata and place under the hot grill for 2–3min, or until golden brown.

Transfer to a serving plate and cut into 8 wedges. Serve with the dressed salad leaves.

Roast Goose with Scrumpy and Sage

SERVES 8

A 4.5kg (10lb) goose

2 onions, finely sliced

2 dessert apples, cores removed, roughly chopped

2 cooking apples, cores removed, roughly chopped

A large bunch of sage

2 tsp sea salt

1 tbsp sunflower oil

Grated zest of 1 orange

600ml (1 pint/2½ cups) scrumpy or dry cider

2–3 tbsp plain flour

300–450ml (½–¾ pint/1½–2 cups) chicken stock

Heat the oven to 190°C (375°F/gas mark 5).

Remove any fat from inside the goose and prick the skin around the breast and at the base of the parson's nose with the prongs of a fork.

Stuff the goose with half of the onions and apples and the sage and place it in a large roasting tin.

Rub the salt and oil over the flesh and sprinkle the remaining onion and apple and the orange zest around the base of the goose.

Roast for 45min, then remove from the oven and pour away the excess fat from around the bird. Pour the cider around the base and, covering the goose with a large sheet of tin foil, roast for a further 1½ hours.

Remove the tin foil, baste the goose well with some of the juices in the pan and roast for a further 15–20min, or until it's thoroughly cooked and the juices run clear from the thigh.

Transfer the bird to a serving plate, cover with aluminium foil and set aside while you make the gravy.

Pour the roasting liquid into a jug and skim off 2–3 tbsp of the oil that rises to the surface. Skim off the remaining fat and use to roast any vegetables. Strain the liquid. Return the 2–3 tbsp oil to the roasting tin, add the flour and stir well. Gradually add the stock and the skimmed pan juices to the roasting tin, still stirring, then bring to the boil and simmer for 3–4min until the gravy becomes syrupy. Season to taste with salt and black pepper and strain the gravy into a jug.

To serve, carve the goose and hand the sauce separately.

Baked Pumpkin

This recipe works well using butternut squash instead of pumpkin. It makes an effective centrepiece for the table, too.

SERVES 8

2 medium pumpkins or butternut squash, weighing approximately 675g (1½lb)

55g (2oz/¼ cup) butter

2 tsp grated nutmeg

4 bay leaves

4 sprigs of thyme

Heat the oven to 180°C (350°F/gas mark 4).

Cut off the tops of the pumpkins and set aside. Scoop the seeds and pith from the centre of the pumpkins, separate out the seeds and place them on a baking sheet. Discard the pith.

Melt the butter in a saucepan, add the nutmeg and cook over a low heat for 1–2min. Brush the inside of the pumpkins with the nutmeg butter, spooning any remaining butter into the bottom. Divide the bay leaves and thyme between the centres of each, then replace the tops. Wrap the pumpkins in foil, place on the baking sheet with the seeds and bake for 45min, or until tender.

To serve, take the pumpkins to the table, scoop the flesh from the centre of the shell and sprinkle with the baked seeds.

Celeriac Fritters

These fritters also make a fantastic canapé.

SERVES 8

2 celeriac, weighing about 675g (1½lb) in total, peeled

A slice of lemon

3 tbsp flour

A pinch of cayenne pepper

2 eggs, beaten

170g (6oz/1½ cups) fresh white breadcrumbs

1 tbsp caraway seeds

1 tbsp ground coriander

A little sunflower oil

Cut the celeriac into thick slices and then into triangles. Cook in boiling, salted water with the slice of lemon for 10–12min, or until just tender. Drain and pat dry with absorbent kitchen paper.

Season the flour with salt, pepper and a pinch of cayenne pepper. Season the breadcrumbs with the caraway seeds and coriander.

Roll the cooked celeriac in the flour, then the egg and, finally, the breadcrumbs to coat. Arrange in a single layer on a plate until you are ready to cook.

Heat the oil until a test piece of bread browns within 30 seconds. Fry the celeriac until the crust is lightly browned, then drain on kitchen paper and season with a little salt and freshly ground black pepper. Serve immediately.

Victoria Plum Clafoutis

Clafoutis is a classic French harvest dish, traditionally made with cherries.

SERVES 8

12 Victoria plums, cut in half and stoned

300ml (½ pint/1½ cups) apple juice

2 tbsp brandy (optional)

425ml (¾ pint/2 cups) double cream

150ml (¼ pint/⅝ cup) milk

2 cinnamon sticks

8 large eggs

110g (4oz/½ cup) caster sugar

3 level tbsp flour

2 tsp vanilla essence

Heat the oven to 190°C (375°F/gas mark 5). Lightly butter a large gratin dish.

Place the plums and apple juice in a large saucepan, bring to the boil, lower the heat and poach for 5–7min, or until the fruit begins to soften. Transfer it to the gratin dish with a slotted spoon. Boil the juice until it is reduced to a sticky glaze, and add the brandy. Set aside.

Heat the cream, milk and cinnamon sticks together to scalding point, then remove from the heat and leave to infuse for 5min.

Cream the eggs, sugar, flour and vanilla essence together until smooth, strain on the cooling cream mixture and pour over the plums in the gratin dish.

Bake in the centre of the oven for 35–40min, or until the clafoutis is golden brown and puffed up. Spoon the fruit glaze over the top and serve.

MARTINMAS

AND REMEMBRANCE DAY

Martinmas, the feast of St Martin of Tours, is held on 11 November. St Martin was a monk and then a bishop in France during the fourth century. He was a soldier in the Roman army for a time and was eventually imprisoned because of his faith. As well as being the patron saint of beggars, he is the patron of many churches; but his life revolved around Tours, where his relics can be found.

The church feast for St Martin coincided with the beginning of the old Celtic winter, which was the ritual day to slaughter all but the necessary livestock. The meat from the slaughtered beasts was then cured and salted to provide food for the winter, and livestock to be kept through the winter would be turned on to stubble to feed. It is traditional to eat roast beef on the feast of St Martin. Martinmas was an agricultural 'year end' of tying up loose ends and planning for the winter and the following year. In some parts of the country the winter hiring fairs took place at Martinmas rather than Michaelmas.

A minute's silence is held on the eleventh hour of the eleventh day of the eleventh month to remember those who gave their lives during the two world wars. Remembrance Day is commemorated in church on the Sunday nearest to 11 November.

MARTINMAS DINNER

SERVES 4

Wild Mushroom and Sage Gougères
Roast Sirloin of Beef with Garlic and Anchovy Jus
Skewered Jackets
Glazed Jerusalem Artichokes
Baked Marrow with Pumpkin Seeds
Autumn Fruit and Florentine Trifle

To accompany, serve a Rhône red, such as a Gigondas.

Wild Mushroom and Sage Gougères

SERVES 4

¹/₃ quantity choux pastry used for Croquembouche (see page 172)

55g (2oz/¹/₃ cup) mature Cheddar or Red Leicester cheese, grated

¹/₂ tsp Dijon mustard

A pinch of cayenne pepper

30g (1oz/¹/₈ cup) butter

450g (1lb/4 cups) wild mushrooms, wiped and sliced

1 clove garlic, crushed

1 tbsp chopped sage

150ml (¹/₄ pint/⁵/₈ cup) crème fraîche

1 tbsp freshly grated Parmesan cheese

Heat the oven to 200°C (400°F/gas mark 6).

Mix the choux pastry with the Cheddar cheese, mustard and cayenne pepper. Fill a piping bag, fitted with a 1cm (¹/₂in) plain nozzle, with the pastry and pipe around the sides of four lightly greased ramekin dishes. Chill until required.

Heat the butter in a saucepan and sauté the mushrooms for 2–3min, then add the garlic and sage and cook for a further 1min. Stir in the crème fraîche, bring to the boil and remove from the heat. Season to taste with salt and black pepper, and keep warm.

Bake the gougères in the ramekins for 8min, then fill the centres with the mushroom mixture, sprinkle the top with the Parmesan cheese and bake for a further 7–8min, or until the choux pastry is well risen and the filling is piping hot. Serve immediately.

Roast Sirloin Beef with Garlic and Anchovy Jus

Most roast meats are usually better cooked on the bone. However, this makes them harder to carve, so this recipe uses a rolled joint.

SERVES 6

1.35kg (3lb) rolled sirloin joint

4 cloves garlic, thickly sliced

2 tbsp sunflower oil

300ml (½ pint/1¼ cups) dry red wine

300ml (½ pint/1¼ cups) well flavoured beef stock

2–3 tsp arrowroot

4 anchovy fillets, chopped

4 tbsp double cream

4 tbsp creamed horseradish

1 tbsp tomato purée

Heat the oven to 200°C (400°F/gas mark 6).

Season the sirloin with salt and black pepper and slip the slices of garlic under the fat.

Heat the oil in a large roasting tin until very hot. Place the beef in the tin and baste with the hot oil. Roast for 30min, then baste with more oil. Pour the red wine around the joint and cook for a further 20–25min.

Remove the meat from the oven and transfer to a carving plate.

Pour the juices into a jug and skim away any excess fat. Pour the remaining liquid back into a saucepan with the beef stock, bring to the boil and simmer for 7–10min, or until well reduced and richly flavoured.

Blend the arrowroot with a little water and stir it into the still simmering jus with the anchovies and cream. Season to taste with salt and freshly ground black pepper, and simmer for a further 2–3min, or until syrupy.

Mix the horseradish and tomato purée together and spoon into a small bowl. Pour the jus into a jug and serve with the meat, handing the tomato horseradish separately.

Skewered Jackets

SERVES 4

2 large baking potatoes

8 bay leaves

1 large red onion, cut into
8 wedges

1 tbsp virgin olive oil

4 skewers

Heat the oven to 190°C (375°F/gas mark 5).

Scrub the potatoes and cut each into quarters. Thread the potatoes, bay leaves and onions on to four metal skewers. Drizzle the oil over the top and season very well with salt and freshly ground black pepper.

Arrange on a baking sheet and bake for 45min, or until the potatoes are tender. Serve on the skewers.

Glazed Jerusalem Artichokes

SERVES 4

450g (1lb) Jerusalem artichokes

250ml (8fl oz/1 cup) chicken or
vegetable stock

4 cloves garlic, peeled and left
whole

15g (¹/₂oz/¹/₁₆ cup) butter

Peel the artichokes and place them in a saucepan with the rest of the ingredients. Season lightly with salt and black pepper.

Bring to the boil and simmer for 15–20min, or until the artichokes are tender. Transfer to a serving dish and keep warm.

Reduce the cooking liquid to 3–4 tbsp by boiling it rapidly. Check the seasoning and spoon the sauce over the artichokes. Serve immediately.

Baked Marrow with Pumpkin Seeds

SERVES 4

1kg (2.2lb) marrow, peeled

2 tbsp roasted pumpkin seed oil

1 tbsp soy sauce

2 tbsp pumpkins seeds

Heat the oven to 190°C (375°F/gas mark 5).

Thickly slice the marrow and remove the seeds. Arrange the slices on a large baking sheet.

Mix together the pumpkin oil and soy sauce. Season with plenty of freshly ground black pepper and brush the oil on to the marrow. Sprinkle the pumpkin seeds over the top. Bake for 20–25min, or until the marrow is tender, and serve immediately.

Autumn Fruit and Florentine Trifle

To prepare this a little in advance, follow the recipe until you've layered the fruit and yoghurt mixture, then add the biscuits just before serving, so they don't go too soft.

SERVES 4

675g (1¹/₂lb/3 cups) autumn fruit, such as dessert apples, pears and plums

110g (4oz/¹/₂ cup) granulated sugar

1 large stick of cinnamon

¹/₂ tsp Chinese five-spice mix

600ml (1 pint/2¹/₂ cups) water

5 tbsp Poire William liqueur (optional)

8 small Florentine (or similar) biscuits

225g (8oz/1 cup) mascarpone cheese

300ml (¹/₂ pint/1¹/₄ cup) Greek yoghurt

Demerara sugar

Peel, core and slice the apples or pears. Cut in half and stone the plums.

Heat the sugar, cinnamon, spices and water in a large saucepan, bring to the boil and simmer for 5min.

Add the fruit, cover the pan and poach over a very low heat for 20–30min, or until the fruit is soft.

Remove the fruit from the syrup and transfer to a large serving bowl. Reduce the syrup to 300ml (¹/₂ pint) by boiling it rapidly, then remove it from the heat and add the liqueur. Remove the cinnamon stick, pour the syrup over the fruit and allow to cool completely.

Arrange the Florentine biscuits around the edge of the bowl. Mix together the mascarpone cheese and yoghurt, and spoon it on to the fruit, leaving most of each biscuit showing. Sprinkle the sugar over the top and chill for 30min before serving.

ALL HALLOWS' EVE/ALL SAINTS' DAY

Halloween on 31 October, although included in the church calendar as All Hallows' Eve, has long been associated with the end of the Celtic year. The pagan feast was based upon the belief that the dead came to life during this time and walked among the living. Old rituals were rife, including the lighting of a candle after dark and leaving it in the window to welcome home family past. Like many of the old Celtic festivals, this was adapted by the Church to commemorate the life of Christ. All Hallows' Eve is kept in remembrance of all the saints.

The two following days, 1 and 2 November, are All Saints' Day and All Souls' Day. On All Saints' Day the saints are once more commemorated; on All Souls' Day we remember all those who have passed away. It is around this time that the church year draws to an end and a new one begins.

In the UK Guy Fawkes' Night or Bonfire Night follows closely, on 5 November, commemorating the plot by Guy Fawkes to blow up the Houses of Parliament. The event is usually celebrated with a roaring bonfire, followed by fireworks.

Halloween and Bonfire Night are among the most popular festivals in the UK and have become a perfect time for children's parties. Although their focus on goodness and God's everlasting protection has become overshadowed, it is an opportunity for children to understand that God is a protective force of good against the dark acts of evil. Our celebration of these two events is a bonfire party: fire symbolizes many things, but essentially the victory of light over darkness.

BONFIRE PARTY

SERVES 12

Bonfire Jackets
Frogs-in-a-hole
Pear and Honey Firework Parcels
Angel-frosted Jam Tarts
Hot Frothing Marshmallow Chocolate

Bonfire Jackets

Traditionally, on Guy Fawkes' Night, baked potatoes are wrapped in foil, cooked in the embers of the bonfire and eaten in their wrappings, while wearing thick gloves! These potatoes can be prepared in advance and reheated in the bonfire if desired.

SERVES 12

6 large baking potatoes

3 tbsp sunflower oil

225g (8oz/1 cup) baked beans in tomato sauce

1 tbsp Worcestershire sauce

140g (5oz/1¼ cups) Cheddar cheese, freshly grated

Heat the oven to 190°C (375°F/gas mark 5).

Scrub the potatoes and then stab them several times with a sharp knife. Mix the oil with a little salt and pepper and rub this on to the skins. Bake the potatoes for 1–1¼ hours, or until soft.

In the meantime, mix the baked beans with the Worcestershire sauce.

Once the potatoes are cooked, split each in half and carefully scoop the flesh into a large bowl, taking care to keep the skins intact. Mash the flesh with a fork and season with salt and freshly ground black pepper, then stir in the cheese.

Place 1 tbsp baked beans into each skin and top with mashed potato. Wrap each potato in a jacket of aluminium foil and set aside until required.

To serve, heat the potatoes in the oven (or the bonfire embers) for 15–20min, or until hot, then leave to stand for 15min. Serve them in their foil jackets, taking care that they're not too hot to be handled.

Frogs-in-a-hole

Toad-in-the-hole is an all-time favourite comfort meal, and these individual 'frogs' are easy to handle with your fingers. They can also be made in advance and reheated for 15–20min when required.

MAKES 12

12 cocktail sausages

55g (2oz/^{1}/3 cup) plain flour

1 whole egg

150ml (^{1}/4 pint/^{5}/8 cup) skimmed milk

1 tbsp sunflower oil

A pinch of paprika

1 tbsp dried oregano

3 tbsp tomato ketchup

^{1}/2 tsp Dijon mustard

Heat the oven to 200°C (400°F/gas mark 6).

Place the sausages in a roasting tin and roast for 15–20min, or until brown and cooked thoroughly. Transfer to absorbent kitchen paper to drain, and set aside.

To make the batter, sift the flour into a small bowl, make a well in the centre and add the egg and a splash of milk. Stir to mix, gradually incorporating the flour. As the mixture begins to thicken, add more milk and, finally, 1 tsp of the oil. The batter should be smooth and the consistency of single cream. Add the paprika and oregano, and season with salt and black pepper. Cover and chill for 15min before use.

Mix the tomato ketchup with the mustard.

Divide the remaining oil between the moulds of a 12-bun tin. Heat in the oven for 1–2min, or until the oil is very hot.

Half-fill the patty moulds with the batter, put a little tomato ketchup mixture on top and add a cooked sausage.

Bake for 15–18min, or until the batter is well risen and the sausages are piping hot.

Pear and Honey Firework Parcels

These parcels can be prepared in advance and warmed through in a bonfire or in the oven. Apples can be used in place of pears.

SERVES 12

6 ripe pears, peeled, cut in half and core removed

A squeeze of lemon juice

4 tbsp runny honey

30g (1oz/⅛ cup) butter

2 tbsp chopped walnuts (optional)

'Hundreds and Thousands' decorations

Vanilla ice cream, to serve

Heat the oven (if using) to 180°C (350°F/gas mark 4).

Place the pears, lemon juice, honey and butter in a large bowl and add the nuts (if using).

Cut 24 squares of aluminium foil, big enough to wrap half a pear.

Place half a pear and a little juice on 12 of these squares, wrap the foil around to make a parcel and arrange on a baking sheet. Bake for 15min, or until piping hot.

Remove the parcels from the oven and place each on a second square of foil to act as a support. Leave to cool until they can be handled, then open the parcels and place a scoop of ice cream on top, and sprinkle generously with Hundreds and Thousands. Serve immediately.

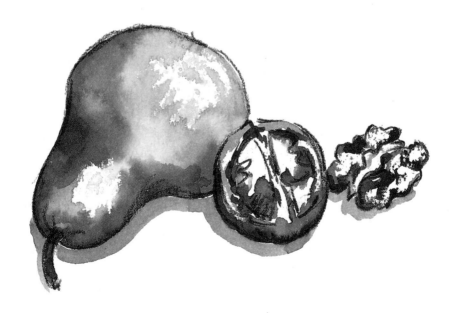

Angel-frosted Jam Tarts

These are sweet and rich, but make a delightful change from a simple jam tart. Classic American Angel Cake Frosting is time consuming and quite tricky to make, so, in its place, this recipe uses straightforward glacé icing – the texture is different, but the effect is the same.

MAKES 12

170g (6oz/1¼ cups) plain flour

110g (4oz/½ cup) butter or margarine

1 tsp caster sugar (optional)

4–5 tbsp cold water

4 tbsp raspberry or strawberry jam

110g (4oz/½ cup) unsalted butter

2 tbsp icing sugar

Vanilla essence

For the frosting:

5–6 tbsp hot water

Vanilla essence

110g (4oz/½ cup) icing sugar

Glacé cherries, cut in half, to decorate

Heat the oven to 190°C (375°F/gas mark 5).

Sift the flour into a bowl. Cut the butter into small pieces and rub into the flour until it resembles fine breadcrumbs. Stir in the sugar, if using, and add just enough cold water to bind the pastry together. Chill the pastry for 10min, then roll out into a very thin sheet. Cut out 12 rounds to line a 12-mould tartlet tin and chill the pastry in the tin for 10min.

Line each tart with greaseproof paper and add a few dried beans as weight. 'Blind bake' for 12–15min, then remove the beans and bake for a further 5min.

Divide the jam between the tarts and mix the butter, icing sugar and a few drops of vanilla essence together. Spread a small amount of this buttercream across on top of the jam, and set aside.

To make the frosting, mix the hot water, a few drops of vanilla essence and the icing sugar together to form a smooth paste. Spread a little of this across the top of each tart and place half a cherry on top, before the icing has a chance to set. Allow to stand for 30min before serving.

Hot Frothing Marshmallow Chocolate

SERVES 12

110g (4oz/¾ cup) cocoa powder

Caster sugar to taste

1ltr (1¾ pints/4½ cups) skimmed milk

24 marshmallows

55g (2oz/¼ cup) milk chocolate, grated, to serve

Mix the cocoa powder with 2–3 tbsp sugar and add just enough milk to form a smooth paste.

Heat the remaining milk in a saucepan and, as the milk begins to steam, use a large balloon whisk to beat it briskly.

Pour the hot milk on to the cocoa mix and whisk furiously until well combined. Return the chocolate to the rinsed-out saucepan and bring to the boil, still whisking, and sugar to taste.

Pour the hot frothing chocolate into individual mugs, drop two marshmallows into each and sprinkle the grated chocolate on top. Serve immediately.

ST ANDREW'S DAY

The feast day of St Andrew, the patron saint of Scotland, is on 30 November. Like his brother, Simon Peter, he was a fisherman before becoming one of Christ's twelve apostles. He was crucified and finally martyred for his faith. He is depicted, in art, holding a cross – St Andrew's Cross, which represents Scotland in the Union Jack. A church built in St Andrews, Scotland in the eighth century became a place of pilgrimage.

The Scots celebrate St Andrew's Day, like Hogmanay and Burns Night, with many traditional dishes, including cloutie dumpling and of course haggis, washed down with a dram of whisky! Scotland nevertheless has a fine reputation for many other foods, including game, salmon and shellfish. A combination of these ingredients makes up a dinner in celebration of St Andrew.

ST ANDREW'S DAY DINNER

SERVES 6

Roast Scallop Salad with Scottish Smoked Salmon
Char-grilled Venison with Chestnut Mushrooms and Rowanberry Jelly
Crushed Neeps and Tatties
Heather Honey, Cheese and Walnut Tart with Whisky Cream

To complete the menu, serve the venison with another seasonal vegetable, such as cauliflower. Serve an Argentinian red, such as a Malbec, with this dinner.

Roast Scallop Salad
with Scottish Smoked Salmon

Serves 6

140g (5oz) Scottish smoked
salmon

1 tbsp walnut oil

Grated zest of 1 lemon

12 scallops

A selection of bitter leaves, such
as radicchio, Belgian endive
and curly endive

For the dressing:

2 tbsp walnut oil

4 tbsp sunflower oil

1–2 tbsp white wine vinegar

½ tsp mustard

Heat the oven to 220ºC (425ºF/gas mark 7).

Brush the smoked salmon with a little walnut oil
and sprinkle the lemon zest over the surface, then
season well with freshly ground black pepper. Cut the
salmon into thin strips and set aside.

Trim the scallops if necessary: remove the thin
membrane around the edge and the opaque piece of
muscle at one side. Wrap a strip of smoked salmon
around each, lemon side innermost.

Wash and dry the salad leaves. Whisk together all the
ingredients for the dressing, keep 1–2 tbsp aside and
add the rest to the salad leaves. Toss the salad and divide
between six plates.

Place the wrapped scallops in a roasting tin, brush
with a little more oil and roast for 3–5min. Avoid
overcooking them, as they will become tough. Arrange
the scallops on the salad leaves and brush with the
remaining dressing. Serve immediately.

Char-grilled Venison with Chestnut Mushrooms and Rowanberry Jelly

Rowanberry jelly, made from the berries of the mountain ash tree, may be hard to find, but redcurrant jelly is a good substitute.

SERVES 6

6 x 170–225g (6–8oz) venison steaks

1 tbsp sunflower oil

55g (2oz/¼ cup) unsalted butter

6 shallots, cut in half

225g (8oz/2 cups) chestnut mushrooms, thickly sliced

450ml (³⁄₄ pint/2 cups) beef stock

4 juniper berries, finely chopped

1 tbsp rosemary, finely chopped

1 tbsp rowanberry or redcurrant jelly

1–2 tbsp arrowroot

1–2 tbsp crème fraîche (optional)

Brush the venison steaks with the oil and season lightly with freshly ground black pepper.

Melt the butter in a large frying pan, add the shallots and mushrooms, and sauté over a medium heat for 5–6min, or until golden.

Add the beef stock, juniper berries, rosemary and jelly to the pan, bring to the boil and simmer for 7–10min, or until the shallots are tender. Season to taste with salt and black pepper.

Mix the arrowroot with a little cold water, blend into the sauce and bring back to the boil, stirring continuously. Add the crème fraîche, if using, and adjust the seasoning. Remove from the heat and keep warm.

Heat a griddle or heavy-based frying pan, season the venison with a little salt and cook for 3–4min on each side, until cooked according to taste. Transfer the steaks to warm plates, spoon the sauce over the top, garnish with sprigs of rosemary and serve.

Crushed Neeps and Tatties

Crushed neeps eaten with tatties (potatoes) are a staple dish in Scotland. In Scotland, however, the word 'neep' (or turnip) is actually used for swede.

SERVES 6

675g (1¹/₂lb) swede, peeled

675g (1¹/₂lb) potatoes, peeled

55g (2oz/¹/₄ cup) butter

4–5 tbsp natural yoghurt

1 tbsp chopped parsley

Cook the swede and potatoes in boiling, salted water until tender. Drain and put the saucepan back over a medium heat, shaking it, for 1–2min to dry the vegetables a little.

Add the butter and natural yoghurt, and season generously with salt and freshly ground black pepper. Crush the vegetables with a fork until broken up, but not completely mashed. Stir in the parsley and spoon into a serving dish.

Heather Honey, Cheese and Walnut Tart with Whisky Cream

SERVES 6

170g (6oz/1⅛ cups) plain flour

A pinch of salt

140g (5oz/⅝ cup) unsalted butter

2 tsp soft brown sugar

1 egg yolk

3–4 tbsp cold water

170g (6oz/1½ cups) cottage cheese

2 tbsp Scottish heather honey

1 egg, beaten

½ tsp cinnamon, plus extra to sprinkle

110g (4oz/1 cup) walnuts, roughly chopped

300ml (½ pint/1¼ cup) whipping cream

1–2 tbsp icing sugar, plus extra to serve

A dash of whisky

1–2 tbsp warm honey, to serve

Sift the flour and salt into a large bowl. Cut the butter into pieces and rub into the flour until it resembles fine breadcrumbs. Stir in the sugar.

Mix the egg yolk with 3 tbsp cold water, add to the pastry and stir to draw the dough together. Add the remaining water if the dough seems a little dry.

Roll out the dough and line a shallow 23cm (9in) flan ring. Chill for 15min.

Heat the oven to 190°C (375°F/gas mark 5).

Line a flan tin with a piece of greaseproof paper. Add some baking beans as weight and 'blind bake' on the top shelf of the oven for 12min. Leave to cool for 5min. Reduce the oven temperature to 170°C (325°F/gas mark 3)

Rub the cottage cheese through a sieve into a bowl, add the honey, egg and cinnamon, and mix well. Pour into the pastry case and sprinkle the walnuts and a little more cinnamon over the top. Bake for 30–35min, or until set.

To make the Whisky Cream, whip the cream until it just holds its shape, add the icing sugar and whisky and mix well. Spoon into a serving bowl and chill until required.

Dust the tart with icing sugar and drizzle with the warm honey, then cut into wedges and serve.

THANKSGIVING

The American feast of Thanksgiving on the fourth Thursday in November has been a national holiday since Abraham Lincoln declared it in the nineteenth century. It is an important family time in the USA and marks the beginning of the Christmas season there. It is held in celebration of the 'first thanksgiving' in the time of the Pilgrim Fathers at Cape Cod in 1621.

A year after their arrival they indeed had things to celebrate. Their crops had all flourished and the Native American Indians had helped and taught them how to survive on the foods that were indigenous to the new land. It was the first Harvest Festival of the New World, with the first crop brought together to create a harvest feast.

The traditional Thanksgiving meal differs slightly from region to region, but it encompasses everything good from the American harvest: roast turkey, the native game bird; cranberries, an indigenous fruit; and wild rice, originally grown by the American Indians. Potatoes and pecan nuts are also a must, as of course is pumpkin.

It also seems a fitting finale for a book about feasts, an opportunity to be thankful for whatever reason you like.

Collect for Thanksgiving Day

Almighty and gracious Father, we give you thanks for the fruits of the earth in their season and for the labours of those who harvest them. Make us, we pray, faithful stewards of your great bounty, for the provision of our necessities and the relief of all who are in need, to the glory of your Name: through Jesus Christ our Lord, who lives and reigns with you and the Holy Spirit, one God, now and forever. Amen.

THANKSGIVING DINNER

SERVES 10

Chestnut and Herb Roast Turkey
Yam and Onion Boulangère
Pumpkin and Chilli Muffins
Roast Garlic and Olive Oil Mash
Mrs Boucher's Baked Wild Rice
Cranberry, Blueberry and Port Jelly
Maple, Chocolate and Pecan Crunch Ice Cream

Serve a Californian Zinfandel with this dinner.

Chestnut and Herb Roast Turkey

The wild turkey indigenous to the USA is always the centrepiece at a Thanksgiving meal. This dish is also perfect for Christmas lunch.

SERVES 10

5.35kg (11lb) dressed weight turkey

2 tbsp mixed chopped herbs, such as mint, parsley and rosemary

110g (4oz/^{1}/2 cup) unsalted butter, softened

For the stuffing:

110g (4oz/^{2}/3 cup) dried cranberries, chopped

1 tbsp cranberry jelly

225g (8oz/1 cup) peeled and cooked chestnuts

450g (1lb) good quality sausage meat

1 onion, finely chopped

110g (4oz/^{1}/2 cup) chestnut purée (unsweetened)

600ml (1 pint/2^1/2 cups) turkey or chicken stock, made from the giblets

2–3 tbsp flour

Heat the oven to 190°C (375°F/gas mark 5).

Singe the turkey with a flame to remove any fine feathers and release the skin around the breast meat, using your fingers.

Mix together the herbs and butter, and season with plenty of freshly ground black pepper. Using a spatula, push the butter between the skin and the breast meat. Season the outside of the bird with salt and more black pepper.

To make the stuffing, mix all the ingredients together in a large bowl and season well with salt and black pepper. Push the stuffing into the neck end of the turkey and secure the flap of skin with a cocktail stick.

Weigh the bird and establish a cooking time: a 6kg turkey will take 3^1/2–4 hours to cook.

Cover the turkey with aluminium foil and roast for 45min, then reduce the oven temperature to 180°C (350°F/gas mark 4).

Baste the turkey regularly during the cooking. Halfway through the cooking time, pour the stock around the bird and remove the foil. Continue to cook until the bird is done, when the juices will run clear from the thigh and the leg joints will feel loose. Transfer the turkey to a large plate or carving board and keep covered with foil.

Pour all the juices from the roasting pan into a large jug and skim off as much of the excess fat as possible. Put 3 tbsp of the fat back into the roasting tin and add just enough flour to absorb it, stirring over a low heat to allow the flour to brown a little. Gradually add the cooking juices, stirring briskly, bring to the boil and simmer, still stirring, for 5min. Season to taste and strain into a warm jug.

Using a sharp knife, carve the turkey meat and slices of stuffing, and serve.

Yam and Onion Boulangère

SERVES 10

1kg (2.2lb) yams or sweet
potatoes, peeled and thinly sliced

3 tbsp sunflower oil

30g (1oz/¼ cup) butter

2 large onions, finely sliced

600ml (1 pint/2½ cups) chicken
or vegetable stock

Heat the oven to 190°C (375°F/gas mark 5).

Season the sliced yams with salt and freshly ground
black pepper. Heat the oil and butter in a frying pan
and cook the onions for 10–12min, or until soft.

Arrange layers of yams and onions in a large
ovenproof dish, adding a little more seasoning between
each layer. Pour over the stock and bake for 45–50min,
or until the yams are tender and slightly brown on top.

Pumpkin and Chilli Muffins

MAKES 8

285g (10oz/1¼ cups) plain flour

2 level tsp baking powder

2 tbsp caster sugar

2 large eggs, beaten

225ml (8fl oz/1 cup) buttermilk

225g (8oz/1 cup) pumpkin or
squash, peeled, deseeded
and diced

1 red chilli, finely chopped

1 tsp paprika

110g (4oz/½ cup) melted butter

Heat the oven to 200°C (400°F/gas mark 6).

Sift the flour and baking powder into a large bowl.
Mix the sugar, eggs and buttermilk together in a
separate bowl. Make a well in the centre of the flour
and add the buttermilk mixture, pumpkin, chilli,
paprika and butter. Stir to form a smooth batter.

Set 10 paper cases in a muffin tin and half-fill each
with batter. Bake on the top shelf of the oven for
20–25min, or until well risen and golden brown.
Transfer the muffins to a wire rack to cool.

Roast Garlic and Olive Oil Mash

SERVES 10

1kg (2.2lb) potatoes, peeled and cut into quarters

1 bulb of garlic, broken into cloves, but not peeled

3–4 tbsp extra virgin olive oil

2–3 tbsp buttermilk

A little grated nutmeg

Heat the oven to 180ºC (350ºF/gas mark 4).

Cook the potatoes in boiling, salted water until tender.

In the meantime, place the garlic cloves in a roasting tin with half of the olive oil. Roast for 15–20min, or until the garlic is soft – don't allow the cloves to brown, or they will taste bitter. Remove from the oven and peel. Crush the pulp with a little salt and freshly ground black pepper.

Drain the cooked potatoes and push them through a sieve, then return the mash to the rinsed-out saucepan and shake over a low heat for a few seconds. Add the garlic, remaining oil and buttermilk. Stir together over the heat until very hot, then season with nutmeg, salt and freshly ground black pepper. Spoon into a serving dish and keep warm.

Mrs Boucher's Baked Wild Rice

Amy Boucher Pye, commissioning editor at HarperCollins and an American, invited me to a Thanksgiving meal and served her mother's famous Baked Wild Rice as an accompaniment. It was so delicious, I've included it here.

SERVES 10

450g (1lb/2½ cups) wild rice

1ltr (1¾ pints/4¼ cups) strong beef stock

1 bay leaf

1 tbsp sunflower oil

225g (8oz/2 cups) button mushrooms, thickly sliced

3 sticks celery, sliced

1 onion, finely chopped

Heat the oven to 180ºC (350ºF/gas mark 4).

Rinse the rice thoroughly and place it in a large ovenproof casserole with the beef stock. Season lightly with salt and black pepper and add the bay leaf. Bake for 30min.

When the rice has been cooking for 20min, heat the oil in a large frying pan, add the mushrooms, celery and onion and sauté over a low heat for 7–10min, or until just cooked. Season with salt and freshly ground black pepper. Add the mushroom mixture to the rice and cook for a further 30–45min, or until the rice is tender and most of the liquid is absorbed. Remove the lid and cook over a brisk heat, stirring continuously, until all of the liquid has evaporated.

Transfer to a large, warm dish, if desired, and serve.

Cranberry, Blueberry and Port Jelly

This is a light and very refreshing dessert after the substantial main course.

SERVES 10

225g (8oz/1 cup) cranberries

110g (4oz/¼ cup) caster sugar

150ml (¼ pint/⅝ cup) port

300ml (½ pint/1¼ cups) combined cranberry and apple juice

30g (1oz/¼ cup) gelatine

110g (4oz/½ cup) blueberries

2 tsp chopped mint

Place the cranberries, sugar and port in a saucepan and cook over a low heat until the fruit is soft.

Pour 5 tbsp of the cranberry and apple juice into a small heatproof bowl. Sprinkle the gelatine over the top and leave to stand for 10min until it becomes spongy. Place the bowl over a saucepan of simmering water and allow the gelatine to melt completely.

Spoon the cooked cranberries into a large bowl and add the liquid gelatine and remaining cranberry and apple juice. Set aside for 15min to cool.

Wash the blueberries and divide them between 10 small wine glasses or champagne flutes, and sprinkle a little mint over the top.

Pour the cold jelly mixture over the blueberries and fill to within 2cm (¾in) of the top of each glass. Cover and refrigerate for 2 hours before serving.

Garnish with extra blueberries if desired, and serve.

Maple, Chocolate and Pecan Crunch Ice Cream

You will need to freeze this for 6 hours during preparation.

SERVES 10

225g (8oz/1 cup) dark chocolate, chopped

600ml (1pint/2½ cups) milk

8 egg yolks

2 tsp cornflour

100ml (4fl oz/½ cup) maple syrup

170g (6oz/1 cup) pecans

170g (6oz/¾ cup) granulated sugar

600ml (1 pint/2½ cups) double cream

Place the chocolate and 150ml (¼ pint/⅝ cup) of the milk into a small saucepan and heat very gently, stirring continuously, until the chocolate has melted into the milk. Remove from the heat and stir in the remaining milk until blended.

Beat the egg yolks, cornflour and maple syrup together and add to the chocolate milk, stirring to blend. Return the custard to the saucepan and cook over a very gentle heat until it just comes to the boil, stirring continuously. Strain the custard into a cold bowl and leave to cool completely.

Meanwhile, make the pecan crunch. Place the pecans and granulated sugar in a heavy-based saucepan and cook over a very low heat until the sugar has turned to a dark caramel and the nuts are lightly toasted. Transfer the mixture to a lightly oiled baking sheet and leave to cool.

When the pecan crunch is cold, place it in a food processor and whizz briefly in pulses until it's chopped finely.

Lightly whip the double cream and fold it into the chocolate custard. Pour the custard into a shallow freezer container and freeze for 6 hours.

Remove the semi-frozen ice cream from the freezer and spoon it into a food processor. Whizz until smooth, pulsing on and off, then fold in the pecan crunch and return the ice cream to the freezer until firm.

Transfer the ice cream to the refrigerator for 30min, to soften slightly, before serving.

BIBLIOGRAPHY

The Holy Bible – Authorized King James Version and *The New International Version*
Maggie Black, WI Calendar of Feasts *(Women's Institute)*
Alan Davidson, The Oxford Companion to Food *(Oxford)*
David Farmer, The Oxford Dictionary of Saints *(Oxford Paperback Reference)*
Elisabeth Luard, European Festival Food *(Bantam Press)*
Claudia Roden, The Book of Jewish Food *(Penguin)*
Evelyn Rose, The New Complete International Jewish Cookbook *(Robson Books)*
Hugo Slim, A Feast of Festivals – Celebrating the spiritual season of the year *(Marshall Pickering)*
Constance Spry and Rosemary Hume, The Constance Spry Cookery Book *(Dent)*
Caroline Waldegrave and Prue Leith, Leith's Cooking Bible *(Bloomsbury)*

Index